TS

Trainsp

Midlands Edition

Contents

About the book

I came up with the idea for Trainspots after receiving numerous requests for information on particular locations, or for information on the best places to photograph on particular lines. There was no good source for photographic locations, other than the odd, insular, local website. Frustrated with this I set to work....

The range of locations available to the photographer changes all the time. With tree clearance, new lines opening up and old lines being reinstated, keeping up with these changes is a huge task.

It has been a long time in the making but I hope you enjoy this book and find it useful on the lineside or the coffee table. It is the first in a series that will cover the whole of Great Britain.

I would like to thank Ken Carr, managing director of Visions International Entertainment Ltd for agreeing to publish the book.

Marcus Dawson
Hertfordshire
September 2009

HOW DOES THE BOOK WORK?

Chapter Information

Gives information about the traffic flows for the section of line covered. However, these are subject to change without notice and should be used as a guide only (especially freight workings).

Location Notes

Gives general information about the area - the surroundings, the amount of road traffic, the type of people likely to be encountered, whether wellies will be needed.

Public Transport

Since not everyone has a car, these notes give information on using public transport.
All public transport information is correct at the time of writing. Walking times are given as a guide only. Bus services and frequencies shown apply to Monday to Friday daytimes only. Weekend and evening services may be different or non existent.

Bus routes and times can change at short notice so please always check before travelling.
Recommended public transport planning tools are:
http://www.nationalrail.co.uk/
http://www.taxiregister.com/
http://www.transportdirect.info/
or you can telephone Traveline on 0871 200 2233.

Amenities

Gives information on toilets, places to eat and other local facilities that can be reached easily from the location.

Accommodation

Gives information on places to stay nearby, if any.

Photographic Notes

Gives information on the times of day that provide the best light conditions, the height of the bridge parapet, whether a step ladder be useful, whether there is enough room to stand and for a video tripod. What sources of noise would interfere with audio recordings.

Each picture contains details of the time, month and lens so the photographer can plan ahead. In order to make this book, each location has been revisited and checked within the last 2 months and the pictures are representative of the current shot available. If there are any changes they have been noted in the text.

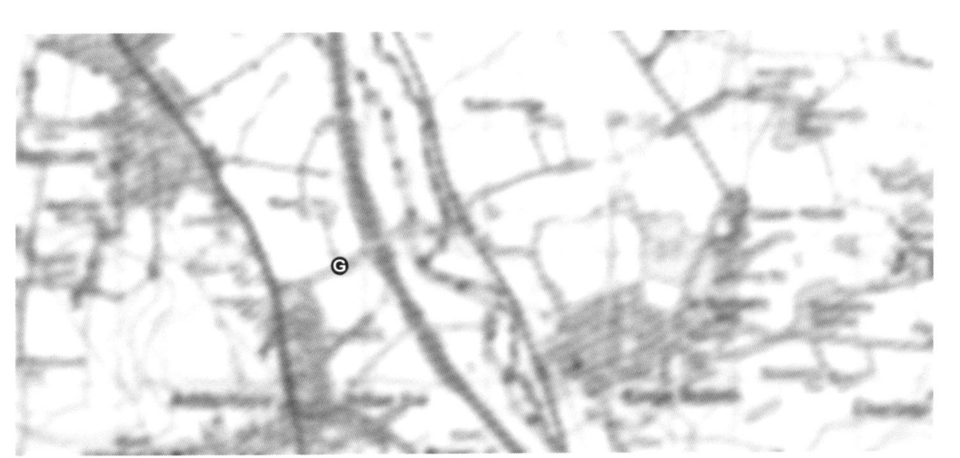

Postcode: X00 0XX **Lat N00:00:00** **Long W00:00:00**

Sat Nav information and Road directions

The postcode provides a reference for your Satellite Navigation system. This will take you to the place indicated by the Ⓖ on the map which will be close to the location. If it is not on the location, use the map for the last few yards. These post codes did not include house numbers so if a house number is requested, please ignore it. They were were checked using a 2009 Tom Tom system. Other systems should provide similar results.

The location is always at the centre of the map and the Latitude and Longitude provide an absolute reference to this point.

Acknowledgements

This book would not have been possible with out help and original input from:

Mark Bearton, Chris Beaumont, Stuart Benson, Christopher Blake, Scott Borthwick, Ken Brunt, Justin Buckley, Ken Carr, Ron Carr, Jason Cross, Albert Dawson, Andrew Duckre, Adam Jackson, John Patston, Les Pitcher, James Power, Sarah Power, Tony Rispoli, Jason Rodhouse,Paul Standley, Richard Tearle, David Weake, Ben Wheeler, Mark Widdop and Iain Wright.

Important Note

Advice about the general environment of each location is given on each page. This information is a guide only. Always be careful. Avoid leaving your property on display and be aware of your surroundings at all times. There are, sadly, people who will not think twice about trying to steal your equipment.

Visions International Entertainment Ltd does not condone trespass and none of the information in this book should be taken as a right to trespass.

The information in this book has been published in good faith by Visions International Entertainment Ltd. All liability for loss, disappointment, negligence or damage caused by reliance on the information in this book is hereby excluded to the fullest extent permitted by law.

Birmingham to Nuneaton

Passenger Traffic

A half hourly (approximately) passenger service, operated by Cross Country, uses this line. It is a shuttle operating between Leicester and Birmingham New Street with an hourly extension to Stansted Airport. At the west end of this section there are also passenger workings heading north towards Tamworth High Level and beyond to Derbyshire. These workings diverge at Water Orton and will normally take the route via Lea Marston.

Normal motive power for passenger traffic is 170s or Voyagers with the occasional use of Cross Country High Speed Train sets.

Freight Traffic

The line from Water Orton to Nuneaton is also a busy artery for freight coming from the Midlands on to the West Coast Main Line. There is coal traffic to the power stations of Ironbridge, Rugeley, Cottam, Didcot and Aberthaw.

Hams Hall freight terminal is just east of Whitacre Junction, therefore traffic to and from the terminal does not pass through the Water Orton locations. Birch Coppice Business Park, and Kingsbury Oil Terminal also lie to the north, less than an hour away. Traffic departing these terminals heads south and must use the western section to access the West Coast Main Line or Cross Country routes towards Felixstowe.

However, some freight workings to and from the north may be diverted via Lea Marston, even if they are scheduled to pass Whitacre Junction. It really can be hit and miss in this respect, and the routing is often down to the signaller's discretion.

Motive power is quite varied with DB Schenker, Fastline and Freightliner providing most of the traffic, but with the odd GBRf and DRS working.

Occasional Traffic

When there are engineering works between Birmingham and Coventry, West Coast Main Line Pendolinos are dragged via this route. Class 57/3s 'Thunderbirds' are usually attached at Nuneaton and detached at Birmingham New Street or vice versa.

The New Measurement Train is timetabled to traverse the route on a number of week days. Serco test trains are also regular visitors when they need to head east to East Anglia or Lincolnshire but these also operate on an as required basis.

1) XC 170102 runs past the Water Orton Crossing
Photo by Tim Easter, March, 13:50, dslr@50mm

2) 66230 heads east into Washwood Heath yards.
Photo by Richard Tearle, August, 14:45, slr@85mm

3) 57315 on a westbound drag through Whitacre.
Photo by Richard Tearle, August, 11:15, slr@85mm

Birmingham to Nuneaton

Washwood Heath

Location Notes

This location is a road bridge that leads to the Alstom complex. Overlooking the DB Schenker Freight Yard, in the inner city of Birmingham, the main lines and the west side of the yard where most locos will be stabled, are visible. There is also a view of the R.M.C Terminal to the west. The road leading to the bridge is off a main dual carriageway, so there will not be many pedestrians in the area. The main traffic across the bridge is lorries in and out of the Alstom facility.

Public Transport

The nearest public transport option is bus number 66 which operates from Moor Street, in Birmingham city centre, to Star City Leisure Park.

1) Cross Country 220 Voyager heads west into Birmingham New Street.
June, 13:15, dslr@45mm

Amenities

There are no amenities at the location. If you come by car you can shelter from the weather as it does get windy on the bridge. There are a number of retail parks in the area with the usual range of fast food and coffee outlets.

Accommodation

The is a wide range of hotels in Birmingham City Centre.

2) With the marshalling yards on the left 57312 heads west.
Photo by Richard Tearle, August, 16:15, slr@135mm

Photographic Notes

You can photograph trains in both directions but you will have to keep crossing the road. The height of the bridge parapets makes it difficult to see what is coming up behind you from the opposite side of the bridge.

Using a step ladder will give a better view over the 6 feet high parapets. There is no problem with space for steps here as the paths are very wide on both sides of the bridge.

Videoing, using a tripod, is possible just past the Alstom end of the bridge as the fence is low but you will not have the best of angles and will have to keep moving for shots from both directions.

Washwood Heath

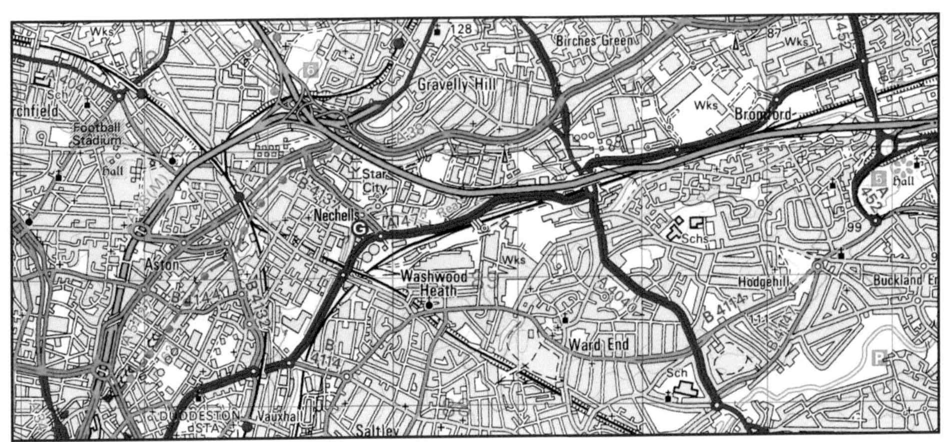

Postcode: B7 5SB **Lat N52:30:09** **Long W01:50:40**

Road Directions

From M6 Junction 6: take the exit towards A38/Lichfield. At Salford Circus roundabout take the third exit onto Tyburn Road heading to A38/Lichfield. Turn right at A4040/Wheelright Road. At the next roundabout take the third exit onto Heartlands Parkway. Continue on Heartlands Parkway and turn left to the bridge as you pass the yard.

You can park your car on the bridge towards Alstom. Your car will be in sight all the time but keep it clear of lorries.

3) With a scrap empties from Cardiff, Advenza's 66841 heads east towards Water Orton.
June, 13:30, dslr@40mm

Water Orton Footbridge

Location Notes

Water Orton is a small but busy village, situated between Sutton Coldfield and Coleshill, and is on the Birmingham to Leicester, and Birmingham to Nuneaton lines. The location is a footbridge which spans the lines with The Dog public house on the north side and a narrow footpath between houses and their gardens and the main road, to the south.

Public Transport

The location is a short walk from Water Orton Station which is served, every two hours, by trains from Birmingham.
In addition, bus service 90 operates every 30 minutes from Birmingham City Centre to Water Orton station.

Amenities

There is a good range of shops and facilities in the nearby high street including a Tesco Express. And 'The Dog' is right next to you down the steps!

Photographic Notes

The bridge has open lattice sides which means that people of any height can use the location. Photos can be taken from both sides of the bridge, and in both directions. Trains approaching from the west on the Nuneaton line can be seen some distance away, but traffic from the Birmingham direction is hidden by the road bridge opposite the station and can not be seen until it is half way down the platforms.
An advantage at this location is the noisy points. They can easily be heard changing, thus giving a warning that something is due to approach from the Leicester line.
The bridge is prone to shaking as a train passes, so perhaps it is not ideal for those wishing to take video footage. The bridge steps should be a more stable position for tripods but if you are using a tripod be aware that the bridge is not overly wide and you may need to move to let people pass.

1) 170113 approaches the station with a working from Derby. *June, 16:15, dslr@85mm*

2) 66589 heads east from the station towards Nuneaton. *June, 16:20, dslr@62mm*

3) 43207, tailing a northbound XC working, takes the Derby line. *June, 16:30, dslr@80mm*

Water Orton Footbridge

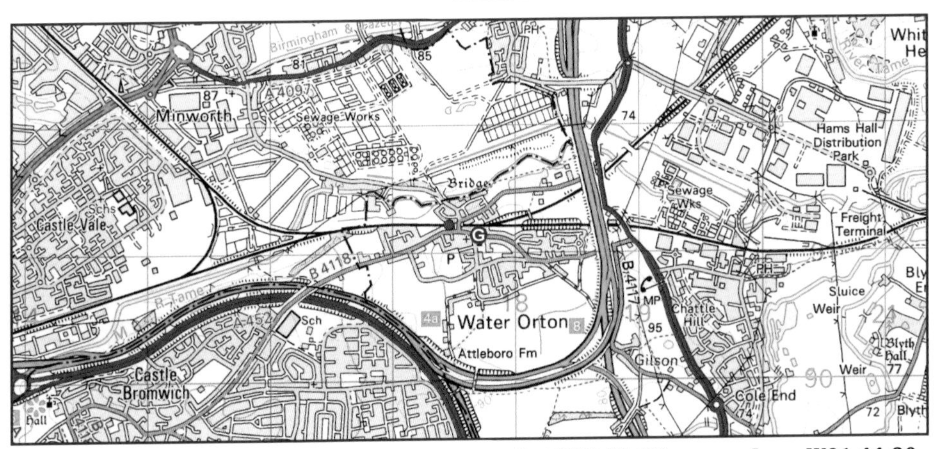

Postcode: B46 1TL **Lat N52:31:07** **Long W01:44:30**

Road Directions

From M42 Junction 9: exit toward A4097/Kingsbury/A446. At the roundabout take the exit onto A446/ Lichfield Road heading to Water Orton/Lichfield. Cross one roundabout. Turn right into B4118/Marsh Lane Turn left at B4118/Minworth Road and you will see the station ahead of you. Park in any of the side roads, making sure that driveways are not blocked. Alternatively, you can park in the car-park next to the station.

The nearby pub has a very large car park round the back, but in 2007 the pub changed hands and the landlord does not like 'enthusiasts' parking in his car park. He has been quite vocal in his views.

4) 66305 with an empty coal working heads east towards the station.
June, 16:35, dslr@40mm

Water Orton Crossings

Location Notes

Water Orton is a busy village between Sutton Coldfield and Coleshill. The locations are on the public footpath that crosses the line linking the housing to the south of the line with the open fields to the north of, the lines. The northern line at this location is the line to Tamworth and Derby and the southern line runs from Birmingham to Nuneaton. The two crossings are a very short walk apart. There is a footbridge over the Leicester line and a foot crossing on the Nuneaton line. From either location you will be able to see what you missed passing on the opposite line. The locations are quiet and the crossings are only really used by local residents walking their dogs.

1) 57006 works 6Z71 Gloucester - Stockton scrap empties towards Burton.
Photo by Tim Easter - March, 13:15, dslr@50mm

Public Transport

The location is a short walk from Water Orton Station which is served, every two hours, by trains from Birmingham. In addition, bus service 90 operates every 30 minutes from Birmingham City Centre to Water Orton station. Turn left out of the station and follow Marsh Lane out of Water Orton. Opposite the last house, at the corner of the field, is a public footpath that leads through the field to the footbridge and then on to the footpath locations.

Amenities

There are no facilities at the location itself but there is a good range of shops and facilities in the nearby high street, including a Tesco Express. The Dog public house is very near the bridge

Photographic Notes

Shadows from the trees can be troublesome in low sun on the Nuneaton line foot crossing. The bridge offers a number of height options from the north of the line. It is suited to either early morning northbound shots or southbound from midday onwards. Neither location is ideal for video, as the nearby M42 is a constant source of noise.

2) On a Stud Farm - Bescot spoil, 60017 heads west from the foot crossing.
Photo by Tim Easter - March, 13:30, d-slr@50mm

Water Orton Crossings

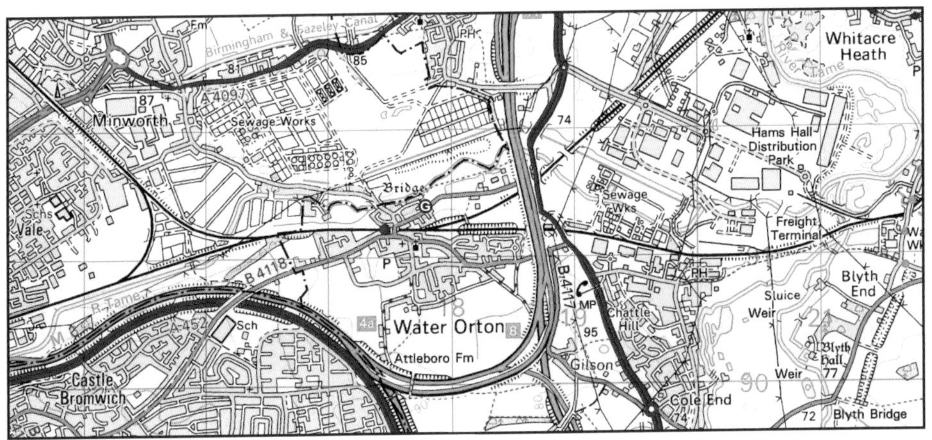

Postcode: B46 1NR **Lat N52:31:08** **Long W01:44:05**

Road Directions

From M42 Junction 9: exit toward A4097/Kingsbury/A446. At the roundabout take the exit onto A446/ Lichfield Road heading to Water Orton/Lichfield. Go across one roundabout. Turn right into B4118/Marsh Lane and shortly after passing under the motorway, park just after the cottages on the left. There will be a lake/resevoir on your right..

Alternatively, access can be gained from the residential area to the south of the lines, via Salisbury Drive.

3) 60040 with a northbound working from Washwood Heath, passes under the foot bridge, heading towards Derby.
Photo by Tim Easter - October, 13:15, DSLR@50mm

Whitacre Junction

Location Notes

Whitacre Junction is where the Birmingham to Nuneaton line meets the line running south from Derby. The location itself is on a large, busy, road bridge between the villages of Whitacre Heath and Shustoke. There is no pavement on the western side of the bridge, only a narrow kerb, so it is not the best place for eastbound shots. Approaching road traffic from the north is on a bend and therefore is not visible to people on the bridge, nor are you visible to oncoming traffic, so do not run across the road on a whim.

Please note that not all freight that is scheduled to pass here actually does! Freight on the line from Derby can often be diverted via Lea Marston, to reach Water Orton. However, any traffic for the Hams Hall freight terminal must pass here as the junction for the terminal junction is just west of the location. The head shunt for the terminal ends just in front of the bridge as can be seen in view 2.

1) 57312 drags a Pendolino east towards Nuneaton.
Photo by Richard Tearle, August, 11:00, dslr@50mm

Public Transport

Stagecoach service 717 crosses the bridge, and stops in the village. This runs between Birmingham International and Nuneaton stations, but also stops at Coleshill Parkway Station.

2) 66003 heads east towards Nuneaton with a liner for Wakefield.
June, 15:30, dslr@28mm

Amenities

There are at least two pubs in the village. Nearby Water Orton has many shops that should provide for any other needs.

Accommodation

There is the Railway Guest House in Whitacre Heath. There is also a large hotel, situated off Haunch Lane, just to the north of Lea Marston.

Photographic Notes

Good shots can be had here up until about mid afternoon in the summer, after which the sun becomes problematic for views 1 and 2. During the 'drags' or when a special is due, this location is popular so there will often be other enthusiasts around. Recent safety improvements to the bridge means that the parapet is now higher than before, so a step ladder is an essential requirement to see over the bridge parapets, but there are lower brick sides at the ends.

Whitacre Junction

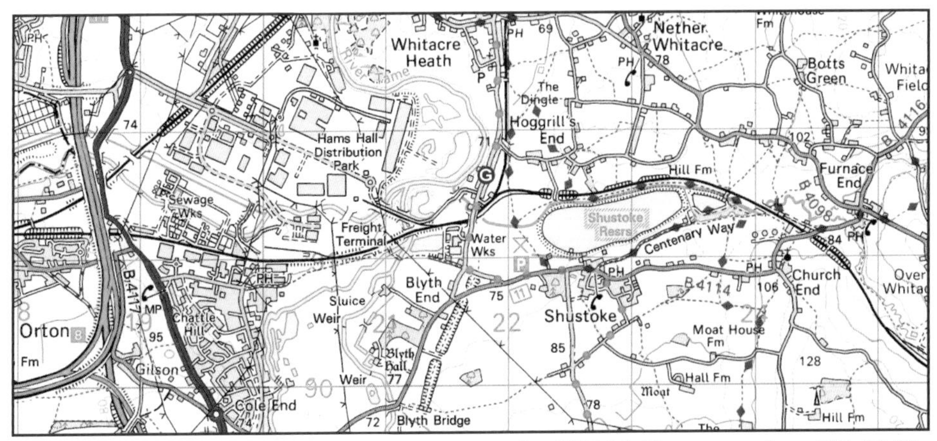

Postcode: B46 2BY **Lat N52:31:10** **Long W1:40:52**

Road Directions

From M42 Junction 9: exit toward A4097/Kingsbury/A446. At the roundabout take the exit onto A446/ Lichfield Road heading to Water Orton/Lichfield. Turn left at the next roundabout onto the dual carriageway (Farady Avenue) and take the first left (Hams Lane) which will take you to Lea Marston. From here head eastwards which will bring you to Whitacre Heath. Turn right at the main road (Station Road) and follow this road to the road bridge. You will have to park at the side of the road, before or after the bridge but please ensure that you do not block any 'work' entrances.

3) 60040 with the Bedworth to Port Clarence Petroplus oil tanks heading westbound towards Water Orton.
Photo by Ben Wheeler. July, 13:30, dslr@42mm

Daw Mill

Location Notes

Daw Mill is an operational colliery but trains from the colliery will not pass this location as they depart westwards just around the curve. This location is a field next to the line on the opposite side of the colliery. The field and it's entrance can be very wet and boggy and the field can be very overgrown at times. In these conditions the location can be either inaccessible or difficult to negotiate.

1) Taken by standing on the fence, 57312 drags 390032, westbound, past the colliery and on towards Birmingham.
Photo by Jason Rodhouse, August, 16:00. dslr@40mm

Public Transport

Stagecoach operates an hourly service, number 717, between Nuneaton, Coleshill Parkway Station and Birmingham International and passes along the B4114 between Furnace End, Church End and Shustoke.

Amenities

There are no amenities at this field location. The nearest towns are Nuneaton and Whitacre.

Photographic Notes

The line runs roughly north west to south east at this point, but due to the slight cutting and vegetation, the favoured shot is of lunchtime eastbound trains. This can be taken with a variety of focal lengths from around 200mm to 300mm from the hill or wider focal lengths from the fence line. A step ladder can be helpful to gain a little extra height to get the whole train in. The vegetation can be quite tall at some times of the year.

Daw Mill

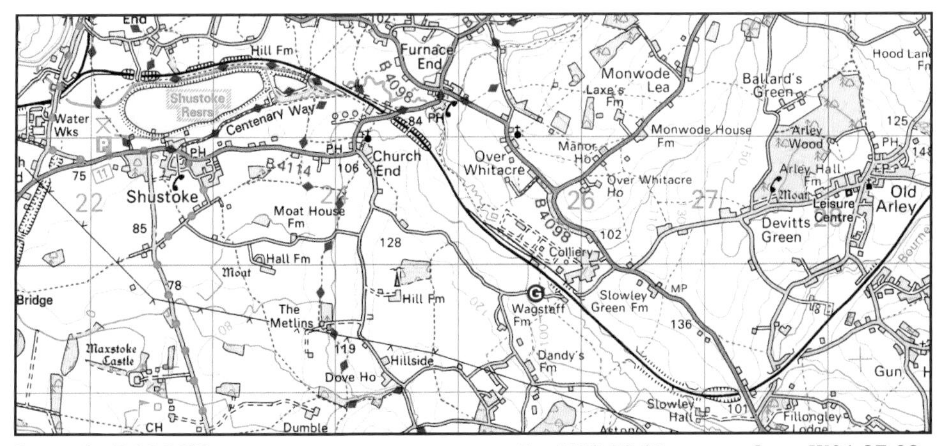

Postcode: B46 2SH **Lat N52:30:24** **Long W01:37:23**

Road Directions

From M42 Junction 9: exit toward A4097/Kingsbury/A446. At the roundabout take the exit onto A446/ Lichfield Road heading to Lichfield. Continue straight at the next roundabout and then exit left at the A4117 (Lichfield Road). At the crossroads, take the left exit up the hill and past the church, this is the B4114, signposted Shustoke. Follow this road, past the reservoirs and over the railway until you reach Furnace End. At the crossroads take the right exit onto the B4098 and pass through the village of Over Whitacre, down the hill past the junction with the B4114 and then take the next right, past the colliery entrance.

Parking is available at the field entrance. Do not block the field entrances or the small road, which is used by large farm equipment. Once parked, follow the footpath through the field to the left until it reaches a small tunnel under the line. Do not go under the line but head off left up the hill. Once at the top of the small hill you will be able to see the shot.

2) 57306 with 390021 on an eastbound drag, powers round the curve on the approach to the colliery.
Photo by Richard Tearle, August, 12:15 slr@189mm

Arley House Farm

Location Notes

This location is a foot crossing between two fields in a rural farmland environment. The field to the south of the line usually contains livestock, whereas to the north of the line the field is arable. If the directions below are followed it is a good ten minutes walk from the car. There is no cover so you might want to take some waterproofs if the weather looks unsettled.

1) 57313 drags a Pendolino west towards Water Orton.
Photo by Richard Tearle, September, 17:45, slr@42mm

Public Transport

There are several buses from Nuneaton and Birmingham International (including 17, 17A and 717) to Old Arley, which is close to this location, with a 10 to 20 minute walk from the bus stop.

Amenities

There are pubs and a few shops in the village of Ansley. The nearest town is Nuneaton which is a few miles along the B4112.

Photographic Notes

The line runs roughly north east to south west and the best shots are from the south side of the line in the morning for eastbound trains, and the north side of the line in the late afternoon and early evening for westbound trains.
There is an acceptable shot from the south side for westbound trains in the afternoon, but there is not really a shot eastbound from the north side of the line.

2) 57308 heads east with a drag towards Nuneaton.
Photo by Richard Tearle. April, 14:15 dslr@70mm

Arley House Farm

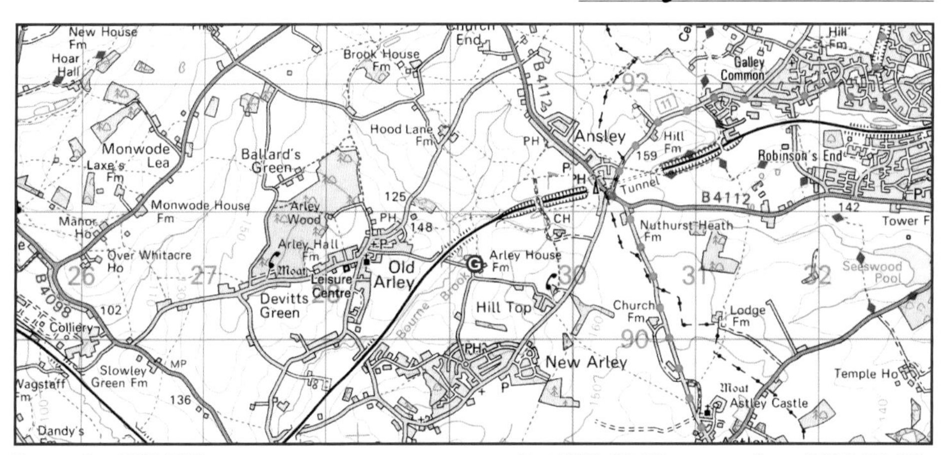

Postcode: CV7 8FX **Lat N52:30:53** **Long W01:34:15**

Road Directions

From Nuneaton take the B4112 westwards until you reach the village of Ansley. In the village take the left turn at the cross roads, which is actually over the tunnel over the line, and follow this road taking the first public right turn past a small village called Hill Top. This ends in a T-junction. Here, just before the farm, there is a large grass verge providing parking space for several vehicles. There is also some parking under the bridge to the north of the farm.

From the parking, walk north towards several houses, between the houses there is a stile and footpath. This can be overgrown with nettles in the summer so it is advisable to wear stout shoes, long trousers and carry a stick to beat them down. Do not be tempted to go through the farm yard – there are big dogs! Once through the overgrown part of the path, you will come to several gates and then into the field. From here you will be able to see the crossing over the railway.

3) 57302 accelerates away dragging a Pendolino eastbound towards Arley Tunnel and on to Nuneaton.
Photo by Richard Tearle, August, 09:10. slr@51mm

Arley Tunnel

Location Notes

This location is the bridge section of a public footpath running between Ansley and New Arley villages. It passes through a golf course and is used by the golfers moving between holes. The line is in a deep but reasonably wide cutting with a tunnel to the east of the bridge. The cutting sides are heavily covered with trees and vegetation during the summer. The area is very open with the only immediate shelter being provided by the trees.

1) 170116 heads a local XC Service east towards Nuneaton.
June, 13:45, dslr@92mm

Public Transport

Stagecoach services 17/17A/717 operate every 30 minutes from Nuneaton to Ansley village with the 717 continuing every hour to Birmingham International station.

Amenities

There are pubs and a few shops in the village of Ansley. The nearest town is Nuneaton which is a few miles along the B4112.

Photographic Notes

Trains can be shot in both directions, from this high vantage point. For the best angle of a train leaving the tunnel a 200mm lens is required. But the bridge sides are low so a step ladder is not required and the bridge is very wide so there is plenty of room to stand. The area is in open countryside and should be free from any sources of noise to interfere with videos.

2) 170116 heads away from the camera, towards Nuneaton.
June, 13:45, dslr@85mm

Arley Tunnel

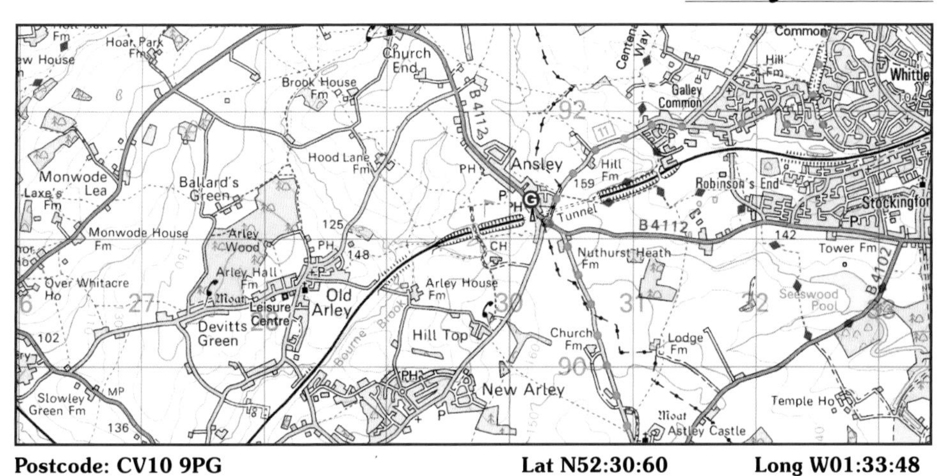

Postcode: CV10 9PG **Lat N52:30:60** **Long W01:33:48**

Road Directions

From M6 Junction 3: take the A444 heading toward Nuneaton and Bedworth. Take the second exit at each of the first three roundabouts. At the fourth roundabout take the first exit into College Street, the B4112 signposted Fillongley. At the mini-roundabout turn left onto Arbury Road signposted Meriden.

You can either stop here and take the footpath from the village over the golf course, or you can continue to the next roundabout and take the first exit signposted Arley. Park on the right hand side of the road by the golf course. A public footpath runs through the golf course, walk past the left side of the club house and follow the main path. You will then come to the bridge over the railway line.

3) 66568 emerges from the tunnel with a west bound intermodal to Hams Hall.
June, 14:00, dslr@200mm

Nuneaton, Grove Farm

Location Notes

Next to the Aldi Supermarket, in the car park to be precise, this urban location is on the edge of a mainly private housing estate. It is known for youths to congregate there, especially after Aldi closes at 20.00 - which is no problem really as the preferred shot is a morning Leicester-bound one. Given the popularity with the local youth it is common for BTP to visit the area.

1) Being pushed by 37423, inspection saloon 'Caroline' heads west towards Birmingham.
Photo by James Power. July, 16:45, dslr@32mm

Public Transport

Nuneaton Bus Station is outside the station, opposite Asda's car park. Stagecoach, service 10, operates a frequent service to Stockingford, and passes the Aldi Store on Kingswood Road.

Amenities

Aldi provides toilet facilities, and of course, there is a good variety of food on sale.

Accommodation

There is none in the immediate area, the nearest is in Nuneaton Town Centre.

Photographic Notes

The location is only really ideal for a morning shot from daybreak until about 11.00 in the summer, after this the sun moves round and shooting towards the sun gives back lit shots. Although you can shoot trains in both directions, looking east towards Birmingham provides a better angle with the view from Nuneaton being tighter and a little more restricted. Not a great spot for video as it is downhill from Arley Tunnel to Nuneaton, so no thrash. Drivers will usually be touching the brakes here, on the approach to Nuneaton, with loads from Daw Mill.

Nuneaton, Grove Farm

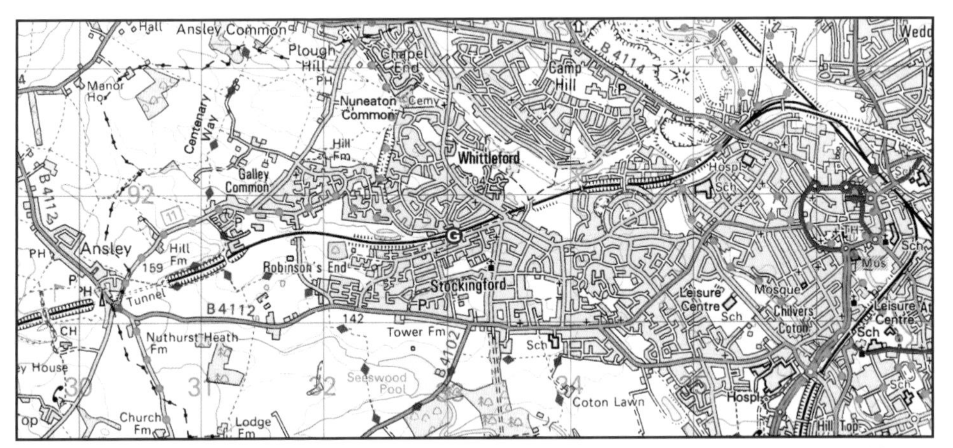

Postcode: CV10 8QY **Lat N52:31:19** **Long W01:30:47**

Road Directions

In Nuneaton, follow the one-way system, keeping right past Netto, follow the road right past the Liquid and Envy Nightclubs and then take the road to the left. Do not take the immediate left as this is a No-Entry. Continue past the Bus Station and at the roundabout by the multistory car park keep straight ahead. At the roundabout by the Fire Station, the one with the fountain, take the second exit onto the Roanne Ringway (A444), travel about ¼ of a mile and then turn right onto Queen's Road. Follow this road for about 2 miles until you reach Church Road on your right. Head up Church Road and turn left into Kingswood Road at the end of the road.

Given that the location is a car park, parking should be easy!

2) 47580 County of Essex slows on the approach to Nuneaton with a Tyseley to Carlisle Vintage Trains charter.
Photo by James Power, June, 08:00, dslr@35mm

Nuneaton, Abbey Street Junction

Location Notes

This location, on the outskirts of Nuneaton town centre, is between a housing estate and open fields. Nuneaton is a very nice and pleasant area but, as with all suburban areas, avoid walking round with your camera equipment on display.

The bridge spans both the original line and the new alignment that takes a flyover across the WCML joining with the new platforms in Nuneaton Station. The new track layout, commissioned in the summer of 2005, was designed to stop Leicester to Birmingham traffic having to cross the very busy WCML. The original curve off the line still remains and is frequently used for diversions.

1) 60022 works a steel train, to Corby, up to the flyover.
Photo by James Power, February, 11:00, dlsr@35mm

Public Transport

Come out of Nuneaton station and follow the road south. Turn right into Newton Road then head down Corporation Street and subsequently Central Avenue. Turn right into Sandon Road and continue to the end. Then turn left on St Marys Road and then right ito Aston Road. At the end of Aston Road there is a gap between houses. This is the footpath that will lead you to the bridge location. This walk should take around 10 to 15 minutes.

2) 37402 & 669 sit with a spoil train on the WCML curve.
January, 11:00, dslr@85mm

Amenities

There are newsagents and a chip shop all within 5 minutes walk. The town centre is not too far away, with Asda opposite the station.

Photographic Notes

Both directions have reasonable angles, but the shot coming off the flyover is best suited to mid afternoon onwards in the summer.

The bridge sides are reasonably high and although caged off, you can see over the top. However, some may find a step ladder advantageous. There is also a shot (view 3) from the B4114 bridge to the west of the main location, of the curve off the West Coast Main Line that is used by freight leaving the WCML and during the drags,

3) 57304 with a westbound 390 drag towards Birmingham.
Photo by James Power, June, 12:00, dslr@66mm

Nuneaton, Abbey Street Junction

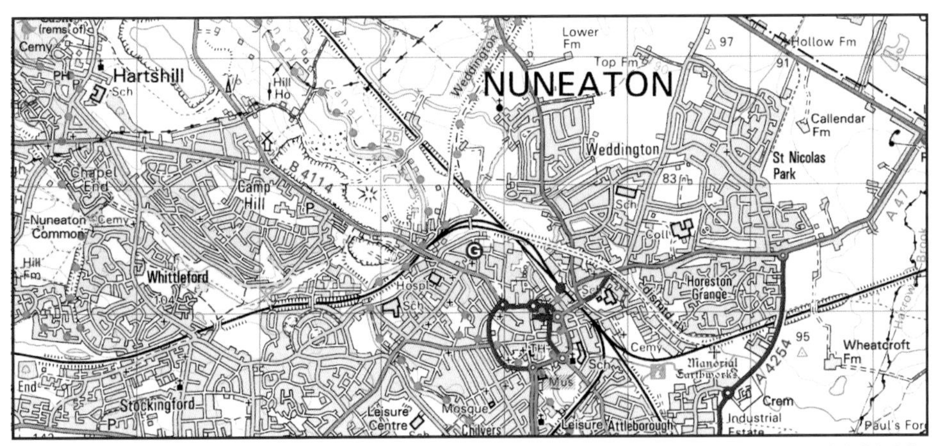

Postcode: CV11 5EH **Lat N52:31:48** **Long W01:28:28**

Road Directions

Jodrell Street is directly off the B4114 (Midland Road) Nuneaton to Atherstone Road. There is a council refuse tip and a few garage type units on either side of Jodrell Street.

You can park on the residential roads and walk to the bridge but be warned the houses by the bridge have no driveways so the streets can be full.

Be careful on Mondays and Tuesdays as they have refuse collections. Big lorries, narrow streets.

4) 60040 heads west with empty steel coil wagons for Margam.
Photo by James Power, November, 12:45, dslr@25mm

Derby to Water Orton

Passenger Traffic

The main operator is Cross Country (XC) although East Midlands Trains (EMT) operates on the northern section of this line. Cross Country workings are mostly operated by Voyagers or Super Voyagers, with the occasional HST set. The local XC services, between Nottingham and Birmingham, usually produce a 170. EMT services, between Derby and Crewe, are usually worked by single 153s.
Just to the south of Burton Upon Trent is the Central Rivers maintenance depot which undertakes all the major work on the Voyager Fleet so Virgin units will also turn up as they go to the depot for maintenance.

1) 43301 at Portway with a northbound XC working.
June, 17:45, dslr@24mm

Freight Traffic

This is a busy route for freight traffic. At the southern end of this section is the Birch Coppice Business Park and the Kingsbury terminal. Birch Coppice sees 4 or 5 trains in and out per day. Most of these are in the hands of DB Schenker, but Freightliner, and in the past, Fastline, also operate out of the terminal.
The Kingsbury Oil Terminal sees around 3 trains a day in and out, operated by DB Schenker and Freightliner. As well as the oil terminal there is a scrap yard which has workings in and out on an 'as required' basis.
Burton Upon Trent has a steel terminal which is served, with a weekly service, by Colas Rail.
There is also a daily DB Schenker intermodal from Southampton.
Passing along the line are frequent Freightliner and DB Schenker Coal workings with various destination power stations such as Ratcliffe, Drax and Rugley. These are complemented by their balancing empty workings. There are a number of oil workings to places like Bedworth and Westerleigh. Advenza operates a Scrap train to Cardiff from either Stockton or Shipley but this runs on an 'as required' basis.
Just south of the Catholme Lane location a freight line diverges towards Lichfiled, and then onto Aston in Birmingham.

2) 60076 powers oil tanks north through Elford.
Photo by Jason Rodhouse, April, 17:00, dslr@70mm

Occasional Traffic

Serco rail test is based at the former Railway Technical Centre in Derby and there are frequent workings passing down the line to destinations in the south. These are often worked by DRS 37s in top and tail mode, Network Rail 31s with DBSOs and there is also the New Measurement Train. This is complemented by engineering trains from Network Rail often powered by GBRf or Freightliner locos.

3) From the Crewe lines the NMT heads back to Derby.
Photo by Richard Tearle, April, 10:30, slr@135mm

Derby to Water Orton

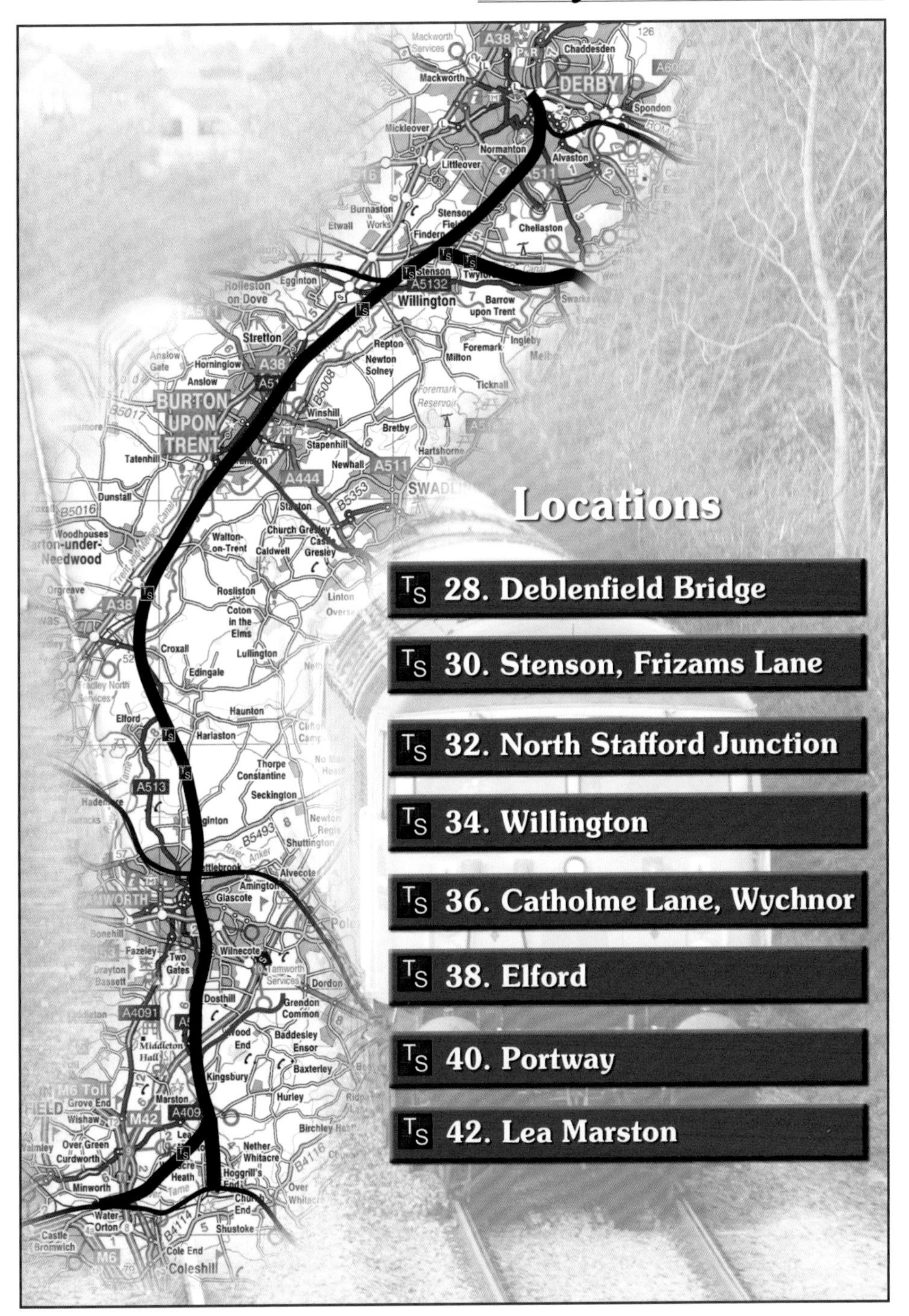

Deblenfield Bridge, Deep Dale Lane

Location Notes

In rural, open countryside this location is a farm track access bridge with a public right of way across the Stenson Junction to Sheet Stores Junction freight only line.

1) 66513 heads east with a Freightliner Heavy Haul Rugeley to Welbeck coal empties.
Photo by Ralf Edge, January, 15:15, dslr@52mm

Public Transport

Barrow upon Trent is very poorly served by buses but Arriva services 37/38 operate frequently from Derby to Sinfin Deepdale Lane, which is the junction at the top of the map above Ashlea Farm, from where it is about a 20 minute walk down the lane to the location.

Amenities

The Ragley Boat Stop public house is two minutes away, to the east, located by the canal on Sinfin Lane. Stenson Lock Coffee Shop is located about a mile along the canal tow path to the west of the location.

Photographic Notes

This location offers excellent views in both directions with the light slightly favouring the view east. There is no real shot from the northern side of the bridge as the canal-side trees are very close to the line, making the shot pretty much head on.

For video the location is fairly quiet with just the usual sounds of the countryside. There is slight noise from the adjacent road and the occasional narrow boat but nothing to cause a problem.

2) 56312 and 311 head an Immingham steel east.
Photo by Ralf Edge, November, 09:00, dslr@160mm

Deblenfield Bridge, Deep Dale Lane

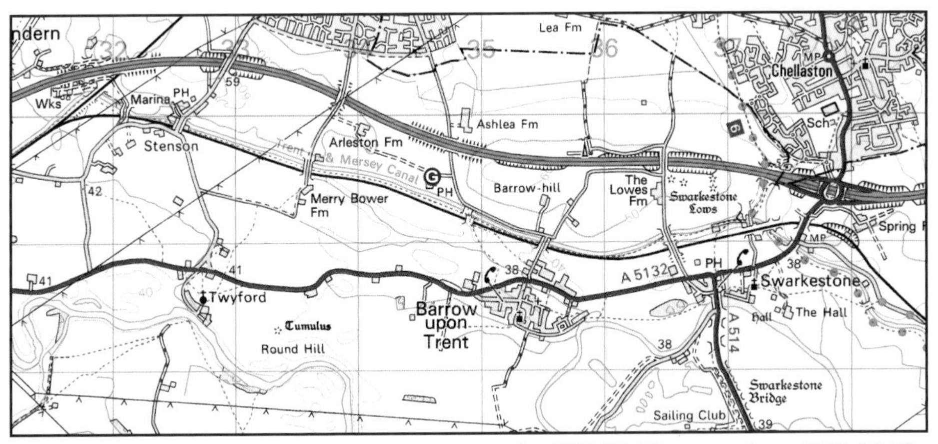

Postcode: DE73 7FY **Lat N52:51:32** **Long W01:28:59**

Road Directions

From M1 Junction 24: take the A50 westwards. Exit the A50 at Junction 3 and take the A514 in the direction of Swarkestone, or follow the signs to Calke Abbey. After approximately ¾ mile the road curves to the left but with a right turn that appears to go straight on – take this turning. After approximately 1 mile take the right turn signposted Sinfin. After crossing the railway line there is a tight left turn and approximately ½ mile along this road on the left is the bridge across the canal.

There is car parking space for two, possibly three, cars adjacent to the canal bridge. Otherwise you will have to park on the roadside verges and walk back to the location.

3) 56303 heads a diverted 4O90 Doncaster to Grain, Thamesport, west towards Stenson Junction.
Photo by Ralf Edge, July, 13:30, dslr@48mm

Stenson, Frizams Lane

Location Notes

Situated in open countryside, with a canal nearby, this is a farm track road bridge over the freight line approximately 7½ miles north east of Burton on Trent and approximately 1 mile from Stenson Junction. This road is only suitable for use by farm vehicles, but parking by the gate is possible, then the walk to the bridge is about 50 yards. It is a public right of way leading to the canal tow path.

Public Transport

Arriva service 38 operates every 10 minutes from Derby to Stenson Fields. From Stenson Road the bus turns left before the road crosses the A50 onto Wragley Lane, from where it is about a 15 to 20 minute walk back down Stenson Road. Walking down Stenson Road you will reach the Trent Canal. Turn right and walk along the canal tow path to the next bridge. At this point walk away from the canal to reach the location.

1) 66301 works a Ratcliffe to Daw Mill empty coal hoppers west.
Photo by Gary Schofield, April, 15:15, dslr@66mm

Amenities

There are none at the location.
The nearest shops are in Willington Village and Stenson. Stenson Lock Coffee Shop is located about 400 yards along the canal tow path to the east of the location.

Photographic Notes

This location offers views in both directions when shooting from the field and is open enough to have well lit angles at anytime of the day. The bridge view is only suitable for eastbound workings due to the line being in a cutting, surrounded by trees, on the eastern side. However, the shot should be well lit until early afternoon, after which the sun will come off the nose of the loco.
The signal protecting the junction is just down the field. Most westbound workings slow down here, or are held for a while, to allow traffic to pass on the main line. Trains will also be accelerating away from the junction if travelling eastbound so the location is interesting for video. Although the nearby A50 is just audible, it should not a problem. Traffic on Frizams Lane is also light enough not to be a problem. You can also watch the traffic on the main line to Derby passing across the field.

2) 170103 & 104 on an eastbound Central Rivers to Nottingham move.
Photo by Ian Ball, May, 06:00, dslr@90mm

Stenson, Frizams Lane

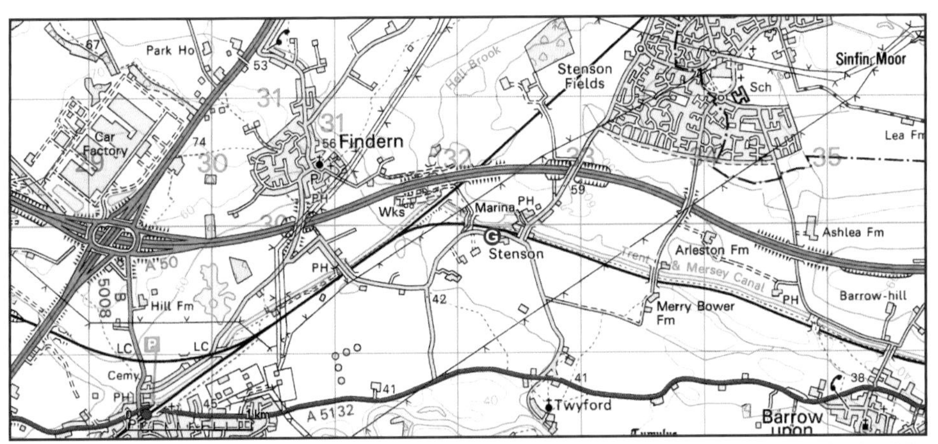

Postcode: DE73 7GB **Lat N52:51:59** **Long W01:31:28**

Road Directions

From M1 Junction 24: take the A50 westwards. At the A50/A38 junction take the B5008 'Etwall Road' south. In Willington Village turn left onto the A5132 'Twyford Road'. Continue out of the village and take the next left. This is Frizams Lane. Head up this road and after 1 mile you will see a gate on the left leading to the railway bridge.

Do not block the gate as the farmer uses it quite often. If there is no room to park, carry on along the road and take the next left turn, park in the Stenson Lock car park and walk back along the tow path.

3) 60044 working a Westerleigh to Lindsey oil tanks east onto the 'branch' at Stenson Junction.
Photo by Ralf Edge, February, 15:45, dslr@34mm,

North Stafford Junction

Location Notes

A quiet footbridge on a little used footpath. To the north is a small field bordered by the Trent and Mersey Canal. To the south is a large area of waste land left after the demolition of the Willington Power station, where only the, listed, cooling towers remain. Spanning the junction where the Derby to Birmingham line diverges towards Uttoxeter and Crewe, this location is often referred to as Stenson Junction. But Stenson Junction is visible, approximately one mile to the north.

1) A Derby bound Cross Country Voyager.
March, 10:20, dslr@70mm

Public Transport

Trent Barton service V3 operates hourly between Derby, Willington and Burton.

There is a rail service from either Derby or Birmingham to Willington but be aware that only about 3 trains a day call at Willington. Exit the station and turn right and walk past the Green Man and Rising Sun public houses. Turn left just before the railway bridge up towards the station car park. From the car park head towards the canal towpath and follow the canal in the Derby direction and after 5-10 minutes you will pass under the Crewe line. Go under this bridge and round the corner and you will approach a wooden footbridge that crosses the canal. Just before this bridge on the right is a gap in the hedge. This leads down to the bridge.

Amenities

There is the Willow Tea Rooms at the nearby Mercia Marina, but Willington is the nearest village and this has a local shop, chip shop and a couple of very good pubs.

Photographic Notes

This location offers numerous shots. The bridge parapets are high but you shoot from the ends which are 'elbow' height fences. The north west side of the bridge is very tight for the Crewe lines, and this will be in shadow during the early morning when the light would have been right for the angle.

Road noise can be heard from the nearby A38 but should not interfere with video too much, especially when a train is passing. If you are planning to use a tripod it would be better to position yourself on the bridge steps. The bridge vibrates with passing trains.

2) EMT 153326 joins the line to Derby from the direction of Crewe.
March, 10:00, slr@110mm

North Stafford Junction

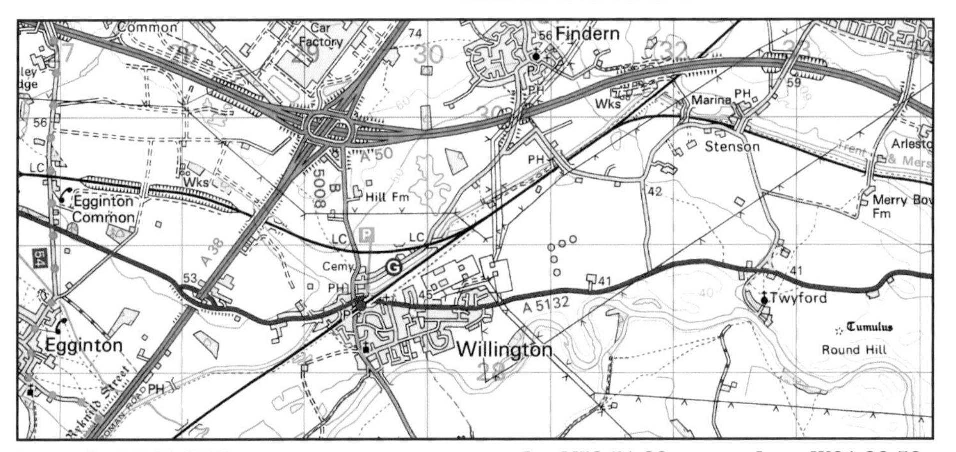

Postcode: DE65 6DW **Lat N52:51:33** **Long W01:32:59**

Road Directions

From M1 Junction 24: take the A50 westwards. At the A50/A38 junction take the B5008 'Etwall Road' south. towards Willington. After crossing the railway turn left and head to the Mercia Marina. Park and follow the canal-side footpath under the road and continue across the new footpaths though the wetlands area towards the Trent Canal foot bridge. Cross the bridge and turn right, walking along the tow path until you reach a footpath, through the hedge, which leads to the bridge. Alternatively, you can turn left by the Green Man public house and continue past the Rising Sun public house. Immediately turn left into Willington Station car park, just before the bridge under the railway line and follow the public footpath to the location.

3) With 43357 leading, a Birmingham bound XC HST speeds south across the junction.
March, 10:30,dslr@145mm

Willington

Location Notes

A quiet footbridge on a little used footpath. Situated in pleasant surroundings adjacent to the Trent and Mersey canal. To the north are trees and the canal, to the south is open rural land. The line is a long straight between here and Stenson Junction which is about 1½ miles to the north east.

Public Transport

Trent Barton service V3 operates hourly between Derby, Willington and Burton.
You can take the train to Willington Station, but be warned there are only about 3 services a day.
From the station turn left and cross the road. Follow 'The Castle Way' road past the general store and estate agent and continue until you reach the first left turn which is Ivy Close. Follow Ivy Close until you reach an underpass on the left which goes under the railway line. Take the underpass and follow the footpath along the side of the railway line until you reach the footbridge. After wet weather the footpath, which is bordered by many plants and bushes, will be difficult to negotiate without getting quite wet. Walking time is about 15 to 20 minutes.

1) 60077 heads north with loaded steel coils. Taken from the bridge steps.
Photo by Richard Tearle, May, 12:45, slr@135mm,

Amenities

There is nothing in the immediate area but Willington has some local shops, a chip shop and a couple of very good pubs.

Photographic Notes

This location offers a couple of different shots with southbound shots from either side of the bridge being favourites. The location is particularly quiet apart from typical countryside noises.
The sides of the bridge are quite high and a step ladder would be required to see over them. But the stair ends are much lower and can be leant on, so there are no height issues. Those areas are large enough to accommodate three or four photographers side by side. Video work should not be a problem. The bridge might shake a little if a fast or heavy working passes by, but the steps should remain stable.

2) A Cross Country 170 heads towards Derby. From the top of the steps.
Photo by Richard Tearle, May, 14:00, slr@85mm

Willington

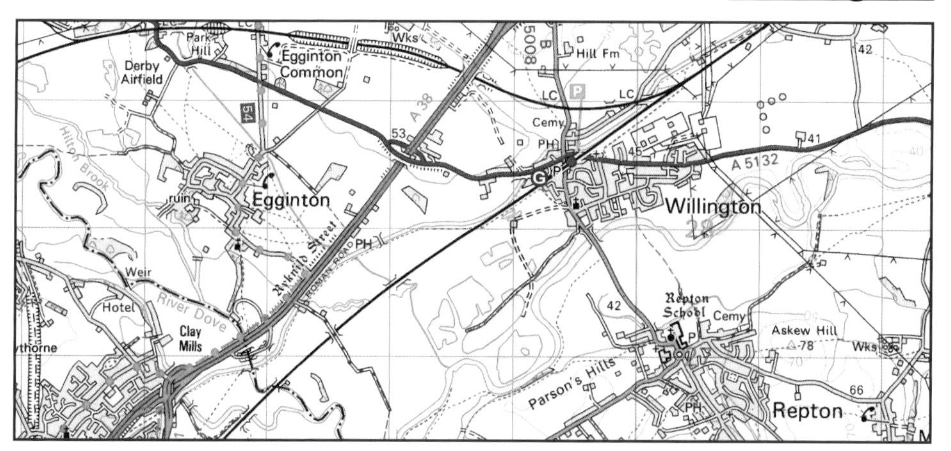

Postcode: DE65 6BS **Lat N52:50:56** **Long W01:34:31**

Road Directions

From M1 Junction 24: take the A50 westwards. At the A50/A38 junction take the B5008 'Etwall Road' south towards Willington. On arrival in Willington cross the canal bridge then turn left by the Green Man public house. Continue past the Rising Sun public house and immediately turn left into a car park just before the bridge under the railway line. This car park is signposted as the station car park. Park here and head back down the road to Willington Railway Station and follow the public transport directions from here.
Or you can park in Ivy Close and follow the footpath from there.

3) Fastline 56303 powers 4O90 south towards Tamworth and beyond. Taken from the top of the bridge steps.
Photo by Richard Tearle, May, 14:00, slr@85mm

Catholme Lane, Wychnor

Location Notes

A back lane road overbridge that joins the A38 to a quarry facility. Just to the south the line splits, at Wychnor Junction, with the main line proceeding down to Water Orton and a freight only line diverging towards Lichfield and then Aston in Birmingham. The bridge is in open farm land. Although it is an access road to a quarry the lorries do not use this route as some of the bends are tight and the quarry has another entrance. Farm machinery does use the lane however, so make sure you keep the road clear.
Visible to the north of the location is the Barton Business Park and on the eastern edge of this is, the Central Rivers Voyager maintenance depot.

1) With the diverted 'Malcoms', having just come off the Lichfield line, 66412 heads north towards Derby.
Photo by David Dawson, April, 09:40, dslr@110mm

Public Transport

Arriva Service 112 runs hourly between Burton and Birmingham, calling at Lichfield and Sutton Coldfield. It calls at Wychnor, Catholme Bridge on the A38.

Amenities

There is nothing in the immediate area. To the north on the A38, around Barton-under-Needwood, there is a Little Chef and a number of filling stations.

Photographic Notes

The line runs north east to south west at this location and is well lit for southbound workings for most of the day. There is little in the area to cast shadows on the line. The line is also straight. There are some power lines that cross the railway line which will appear in the skyline of shots, but should not interfere with the subject matter.
To the south of the location, on the west side of the line, is a large radio mast and small brick building, so northbound shots from that side of the bridge may have to be framed quite tightly. The quarry facilities produce a constant stream of clanks and crashes which would certainly interfere with any sound recordings.

Catholme Lane, Wychnor

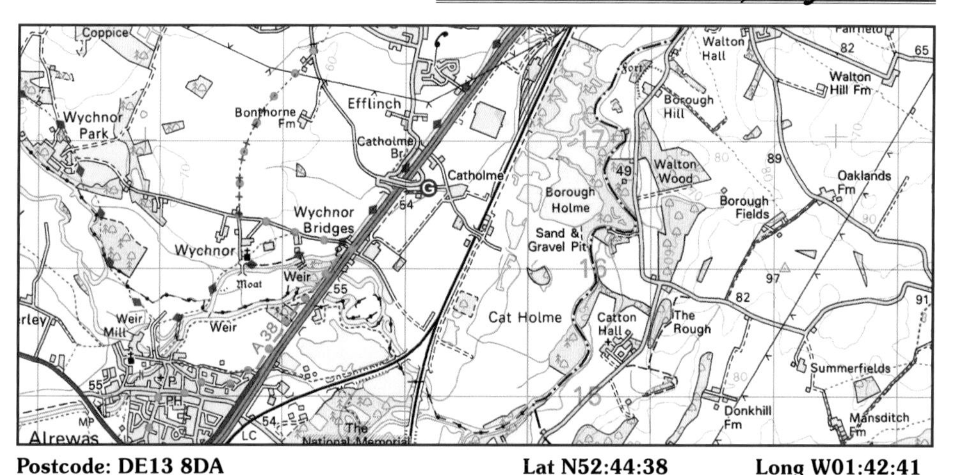

Postcode: DE13 8DA **Lat N52:44:38** **Long W01:42:41**

Road Directions

From the A38 between Burton upon Trent and Lichfield exit towards the B5016. If you are travelling from the north take the first exit at the roundabout and head toward Station Road. At the next roundabout take the third exit and then after about 300 yards, turn right. From the south take the exit to the B5016 and follow Station Road. Cross one roundabout.and then after about 300 yards, turn right. The location is about 1½ miles along this road.There are plenty of grass verges on which you can park, but make sure there is room for other vehicles to pass.

2) 56303 heads towards Water Orton with the Boston Docks to Washwood Heath steel working.
Photo by Scott Borthwick, September, 10:30, dslr@66mm

Elford

Location Notes

This location is a bridge situated in open farmland with the village of Elford about a mile away. The bridge carries a rural road. Although traffic on the road is sparse it can be travelling at reasonable speeds so be wary when standing on the roadside verges.

1) 60013 pulls into the loop with a southbound oil working.
Photo by Mark Bearton, July, 11:20, dslr@75mm

Public Transport

Acorn Coaches of Tamworth operates the 787. This service, which runs roughly hourly in the mornings and early afternoons, starts in Tamworth and calls at Elford Village.

Amenities

There is a pub and some local shops in the village of Elford.

Photographic Notes

At this point on the line there is a freight loop where slower workings can be recessed to allow faster ones to overtake. Northbound workings cannot be seen until they have passed under the bridge to the south of the location. But southbound workings can be viewed in the distance on the long straight approaching the location The light is best from late morning onwards for trains heading towards Birmingham. The line to the north is elevated above the fields though it enters a low, wide cutting at the bridge so afternoon views of northbound trains will be into the sun.

2) 47739/727 depart the loop. Taken from the southern bridge.
Photo by David Dawson, March, 14:30, dslr@40mm

You can photograph from the bridge itself, but there are also footpaths on both sides of the bridge that lead to the fields which give almost side views both at the bridge location and further up the line for trains arriving in the loop.

Elford

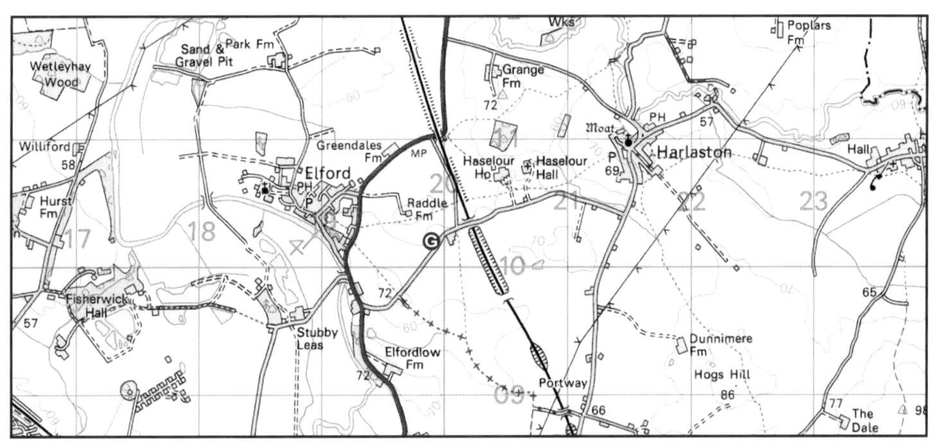

Postcode: B79 9DR **Lat N52:41:26** **Long W01:42:08**

Road Directions

From M42 Junction 10: take the A5 exit towards Tamworth. After about 3 miles take the exit towards A51/ Tamworth. Drive through Tamworth on the A453 and B5493 and leave via the A513 northwards. After about 3 miles, before you reach the village of Elford, turn right along a narrow road. This leads to the overbridge.

There is plenty of room to park on the verges approaching the bridge.

3) 66303, standing in for a Fastline 56, seen here pulling into the loop with a well loaded 4090 Doncaster - Grain working. *Photo by Scott Borthwick, September, 13:15, slr@54mm*

Portway

Location Notes

Situated on a farmers' track overbridge in a green lane environment this is a favoured afternoon southbound shot in the open countryside. It is very peaceful here and the only people likely to pass are walkers and farmers and fellow photographers visiting the bridge.

1) Looking south from the bridge, load haul 60059 takes empty oil tanks back to Lindsey.
June, 17:30, dslr@24mm

Public Transport

Services 787/804 operated by Acorn Coaches provides circular services from Tamworth to Portway and Elford. They run approximately every 60-90 minutes although the last journey to serve Portway currently leaves there at 13.43 back to Tamworth. Travelline Midlands will provide more information.

Amenities

There are no local amenities, but Tamworth town is only a few miles to the south

Photographic Notes

The preferred shot at this location is of southbound workings, Although there are electricity wires which cross the line just to the north, this is a minor inconvenience and these can be easily framed out of your shot if you use a lens of at least 120mm (85mm dig).
It is basically an afternoon shot as the sun needs to be round to the west. The southbound ¾ shot in the morning would leave you little scope, if any, for composition other than a straight, head on, shot due to the trees on the east side of the line.
The northbound shot is fair but you get little notice of trains approaching as there is a road bridge about 300m to the south. The location is quiet and would suit video recordings.

2) NXEC hired in Power Car on a northbound XC HST.
June, 17:50, dslr@24mm

Portway

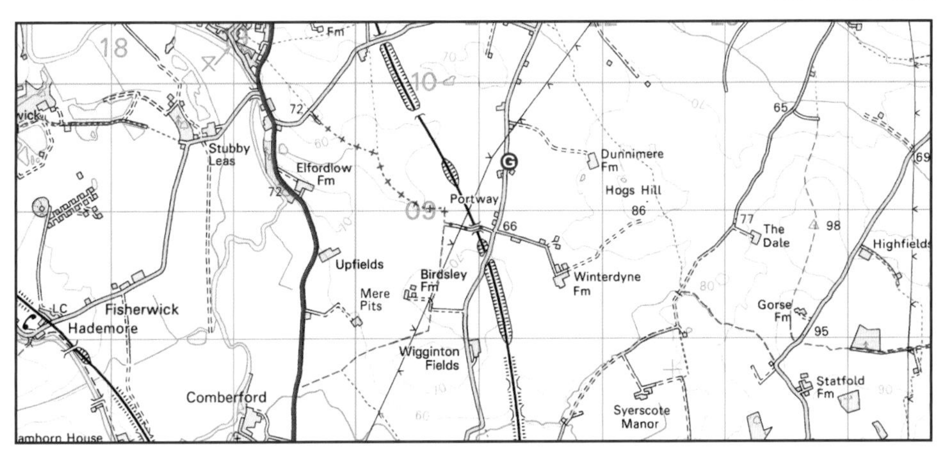

Postcode: B79 9LA **Lat N52:40:38** **Long W01:41:28**

Road Directions

From M42 Junction 10: take the A5 exit towards Tamworth. After about 3 miles take the exit towards A51/ Tamworth. Drive through Tamworth on the A453 and B5493 and leave via the A513 northwards. After going under the national grid electricity wires, turn right towards Wigginton. In the village turn left and head north. You will cross over one railway bridge and just after this, on the left, is the turning to the location's bridge. You can park on the bridge, ensuring you leave space for farm vehicles to pass. However, it is worth noting that turning is difficult on the bridge when there are cars on it and there are no suitable places to turn on the green lane after the bridge, so you may have to reverse off the bridge back down the lane. Otherwise there are roadside spaces on Portway Lane.

3) Heading south for Birmingham New Street and beyond, 220033/07 catches the afternoon light.
June, 17:45, dslr@85mm

Lea Marston

Location Notes

Lea Marston is a village to the east of Birmingham and is on the triangle of lines between Water Orton and Kingsbury. This location is a large road bridge but it is reasonably quiet here. There is pavement on the north east side only, with the other being just a short grass kerb area.
Not all freight that is scheduled to pass here actually does. Freight can often be diverted via Whitacre Junction, which is on another side of the triangle.

1) 66161 heads west with a rake of loaded coal wagons.
Picture by Jason Rodhouse, April, 12:00, dslr@53mm

Public Transport

Stagecoach in Warwickshire operates route 717 every hour Monday - Saturday between Nuneaton and Birmingham International Airport. The bus passes over the bridge but unless you can sweet talk the driver, you will need to alight in the village and walk to the bridge, this however should take no more than 5 minutes.

2) 56303 with a late running 4O90 to Grain.
Picture by Jason Rodhouse, May, 16:15, dslr@32mm

Amenities

There are plenty of amenities in nearby Water Orton, including a Tesco and Post Office. There are also at least two pubs at Whitacre Heath.

Accommodation

There is a large hotel to the north of the village down Haunch Lane. There is also the Railway Guest House in Whitacre Heath.

Photographic Notes

In the summer, good shots of southbound workings can be had here until the early afternoon, although northbound workings are really only suited to a morning shoot.
This location can get very busy if something unusual is due, and though not essential, a step ladder may be an advantage, if only to get above other photographers' heads.
A shot can also be had from a gap in the hedge, a stone's throw to the south of the bridge.

3) Cross Country units pass while crossing the River Tame.
June, 16:00, dslr@80mm

Lea Marston

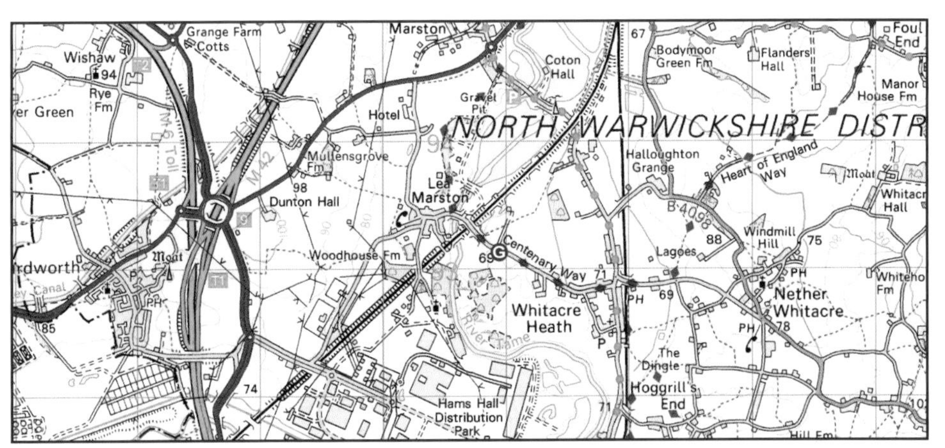

Postcode: B46 2HD **Lat N52:32:14** **Long W91:41:44**

Road Directions

From the M42 Junction 9: head south on the A446 Lichfield Road then take the first left at the roundabout down Faraday Avenue, which is a dual carriageway. Take the first left which will take you to the village itself. In the centre of the village, bear right onto the road which leads to Whitacre Heath. As you leave the village of Lea Marston you will pass over the railway, and this is the location.

You can park just beyond the bridge by the side of the road. There is also room to park off-road on the left hand side at the bottom of the hill before the bridge.

4) 66069 with a Hams Hall to Wakefield Europort intermodal working, heading north.
Photo by Tim Easter, October, 10:45, d-sle@50mm

Peterborough to Derby

Passenger Traffic

On the Main Line, between Derby and Leicester, East Midland Trains HSTs and 222s operate the services to London. These are supplemented, on local trains, by 153 and 156 units. Cross Country operates class 170s at the Derby end of the line using the route, via Trent, to Nottingham, as well as working between Leicester and Peterborough.

1) XC 170111 approaches Derby.
June, 10:00, dslr@52mm

Freight Traffic

There is little traffic between Derby and Trent as most traffic through Derby goes south via Burton and everything else will go via Toton but once past Trent junctions this traffic joins the line. Traffic taking this route includes stone and cement workings from the Peak Forest going to Ely, most of which will take the north side of the Syston Triangle to join the Melton Mowbray line. With the La Farge stone works at Mountsorrel there is plenty of stone traffic with both the standard hoppers or their own 'Self Discharge Train'.

2) 66701 passes Cossington with an NR train.
June, 11:30, dslr@72mm

Occasional Traffic

Plenty of Serco traffic from Derby uses the route to access the Anglia region. Network Rail engineering trains, running out of March Whitemoor yard, frequently run through the area.
With the East Midlands Test Centre at Asfordby in the area, almost anything with rail wheels might appear. Currently, in 2009, it is London Underground Tube stock on test, which is hauled in from Derby Litchurch Lane works.

3) 37610 & 37611 pass Frisby en route to Ilford with a transit move for the overhead line test train.
Photo by Ben Wheeler, July, 08:00, dslr@35mm

Peterborough to Derby

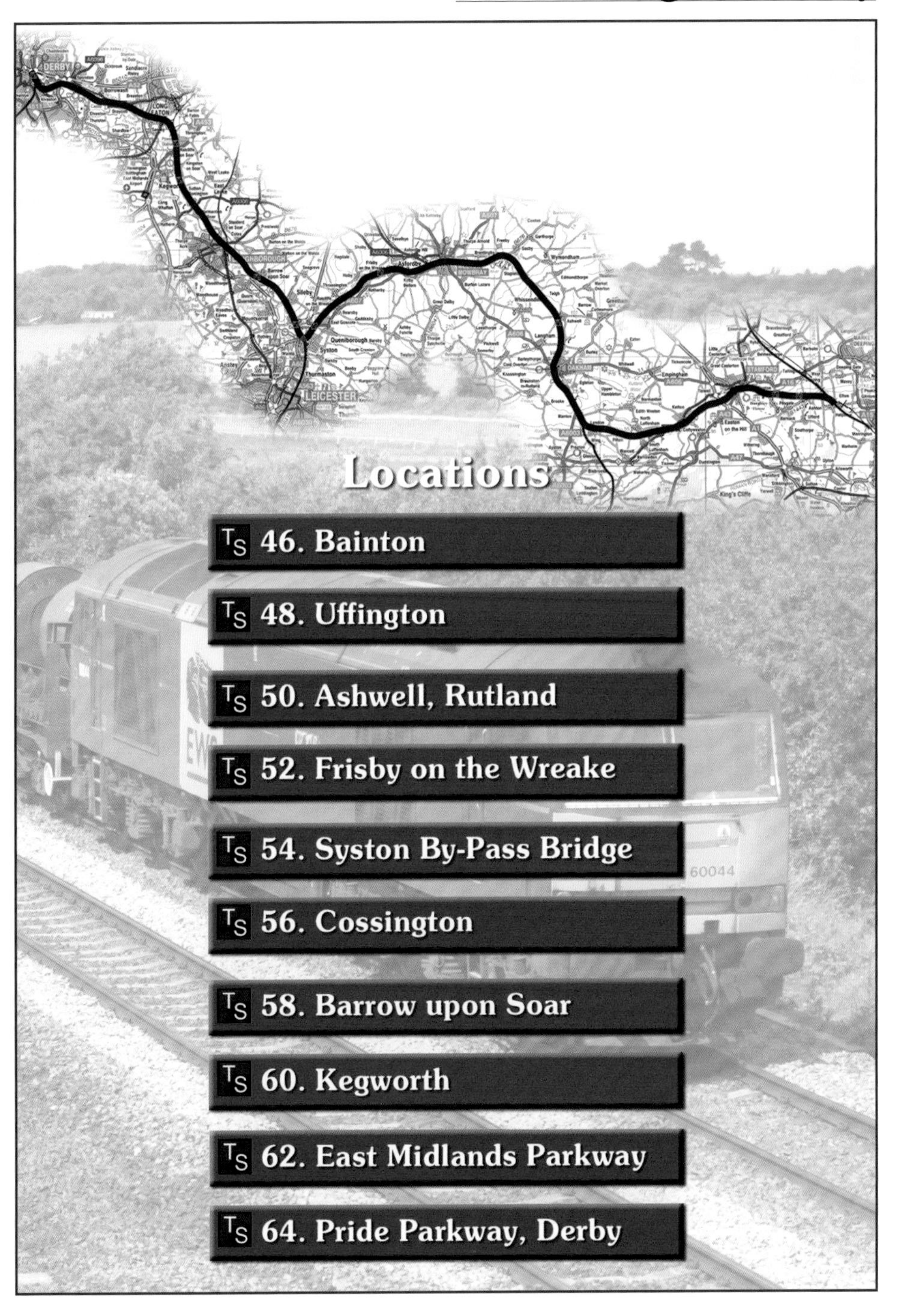

Locations

Bainton

Location Notes

Bainton is a quiet village located between Stamford and Market Deeping, and lies to the north west of Peterborough. The location is a level crossing at the north of the village, in farmland.

1) 170113 with an east bound XC working to Stansted. This view was taken from the northern field edge.
August, 08:15, dslr@24mm

Public Transport

Delaine service 201 operates from Peterborough, Queensgate, to Bainton between 09:00 and 18:00.

Amenities

There is nothing at the location itself, but nearby Tallington has a couple of useful shops and a good inn. Failing that there is a large range of shops, including a Tesco, in Stamford.

2) 170398, heading east, as seen from the crossing's north side.
August, 08:00, dslr@45mm

Photographic Notes

The location is primarily an eastbound shot. Westbound shots can not really be had here, due to the cottage or grain silos blocking the view.
The line runs pretty much straight, in an east to west direction so shots of eastbound trains are best up to about lunchtime.
This would be a nice spot for those who wish to take video. The crossing is an automatic half barrier, but the warning sirens are quiet. You can also see down to Uffington crossing, to the west, and this will give additional warning of approaching trains as the barriers are shut well before time.

Bainton

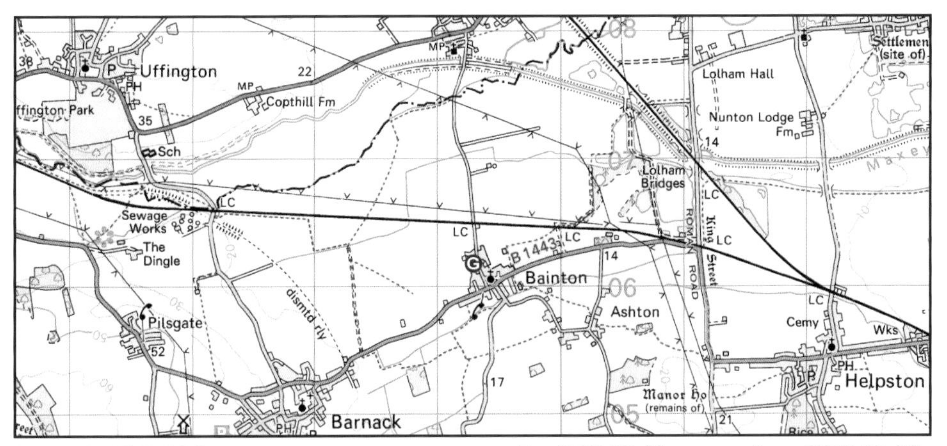

Postcode: PE9 3AS **Lat N52:38:42** **Long W00:23:10**

Road Directions

From Stamford on the A1: head east on the A16 following signs for Spalding. When you come to the village of Tallington, look for a turning on the right hand side, Tallington Road. This road leads to the level crossing.

You can park on road side verges on either side of the crossing, but avoid parking in front of the cottage.

3) From the crossing's southern side 66120 is seen heading east towards Ely, with a stone working from Peak Forest.
August, 07:45, dslr@72mm

Uffington

Location Notes

Uffington is a quiet village located between Stamford and Market Deeping, north west of Peterborough. The location a level crossing and fields just to the south of the village.

1) 170159 heads west passing another XC working heading east. The unit is crossing the Farmers Crossing in the fields.
Photo by Jason Rodhouse, February, 13:00, dslr@42mm

Public Transport

You can either walk from Stamford Station along the footpaths that follow the railway line, or walk from Bainton after taking the Delaine service 201 from Peterborough, Queensgate. Both walks will take around 30 minutes.

Amenities

There is nothing at the location itself but nearby Tallington has a couple of useful shops and a good inn. Failing that there is a large range of shops, including a Tesco, in Stamford.

2) Looking west as XC 170s 518 and 636 pass.
August, 09:00, dslr@30mm

Photographic Notes

The line runs pretty much east to west here, and as such, shots of eastbound trains are best up to about lunchtime, after which the location becomes favourable for westbound workings.
There is a farmers' crossing where shots can be taken to the east, otherwise a step ladder is recommended in the summer months to get elevation above the tall lineside growth. Shots from the crossing itself are quite tight, but the gates are quite large and easily big enough for a head and camera to fit through with plenty of room to spare.
It is not unusual for cross country workings to pass each other around this location.

Ashwell, Rutland

Location Notes

A quiet location on the outskirts of Ashwell village, in the tiny county of Rutland. It is a quiet and safe place to visit.

1) 66506 heads east, across the crossing, towards Peterborough with a Earles to West Thurrock cement working.
August, 10:00, dslr@66mm

Public Transport

From Oakham Station you can take the number 19 bus to the village of Ashwell.

Amenities

There are no local amenities.
Oakham, which is a few miles to the south, has a good selection of shops including supermarkets and fast food outlets.

2) 170112 with a westbound XC working to Leicester.
August, 10:30, dslr@32mm

Accommodation

There are local Bed and Breakfasts in Oakham and Whissendine, within 10 minutes drive.

Photographic Notes

With the line running north to south the location favours an afternoon southbound shot. The only slight hitch would be the lineside vegetation, which will require a step ladder to get over properly. As a bonus there is a semaphore on the Peterborough bound line.
The crossing is an always down type and raises when requested by the use of an 'asking plunger'. But since the gates do not raise automatically a step ladder can be, carefully, set up without worrying about the gates moving. A warning bell rings when the gates are lowering.The next crossing, situated by the signal box, can also be seen, so those gates going down will give advance warning, as will the semaphores clearing for approaching trains.

Uffington

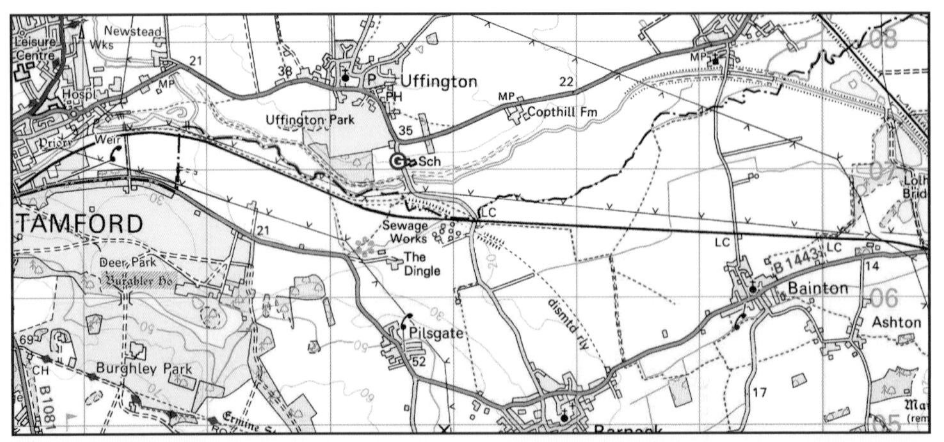

Postcode: PE9 3AD **Lat N52:38:48** **Long W00:25:03**

Road Directions

From Stamford on the A1: head east on the A16 following signs for Spalding. You will shortly pass through Uffington village. As you do so, the main road bends sharply to the left, but you should take a right turn (appears straight ahead) to Barncak. This road will lead you to the level crossing.

Park safely by the roadside. Please do not block the entrance or driveway to the cottage.

3) Returning the High Output Ballast Cleaner to Whitemoor yard, March, 66565 travels east past the Uffington box.
August, 08:30, dslr@24mm

Ashwell, Rutland

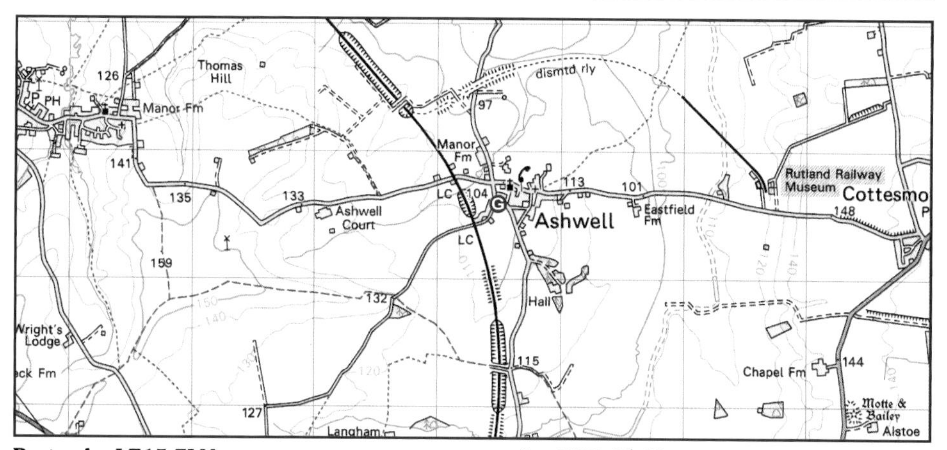

Postcode: LE15 7LN **Lat N52:42:42** **Long W00:43:27**

Road Directions

From the A1 at Stamford: take the A606 westbound, towards Melton Mowbray, and follow this road to Oakham. When you reach the roundabout take the second exit, right turn, to the next roundabout. Here take the third exit, right turn, onto the B668 Burley Road and continue north up this road for about 500 yards. After the playing fields there is a left turn to Station Road then a left turn to Ashwell Road. Continue north along Ashwell Road until you reach the village.

There are grass verges on both sides with room for about three cars.

3) With one of the line's semaphores in the background, 67002 approaches the crossing with the Northern Belle.
Photo by Ben Wheeler, April, 13:50, dslr@50mm

Washstones Crossing, Frisby on the Wreake

Location Notes

An open field location, with a clear view in each direction. It is surrounded by trees and bushes. The village of Frisby is clearly visible from this spot. The nearest city is Leicester, which is situated about 15-20 minutes away, depending on which route you take.

1) 37423 pushes Inspection Saloon 'Caroline' on a Derby RTC circular tour.
Photo by Ben Wheeler, July, dslr@50mm

Public Transport

Paul James Coaches operates service 128 on behalf of Leicester County Council and runs hourly between Melton Mowbray and Leicester via Frisby village.

Amenities

There is an off-license/newsagent in the village, less than a mile away. There is also a pub around the corner from the newsagent.

Photographic Notes

The crossing is an 'R&G' (Red and Green) type so advance notice can be had from the crossing lights. To the west are 'whistle' boards so trains should sound horns on approach.
In the summer the light is good between 10.00 and 19.00, after that it is backlit. The sun can pose a problem from 18.00 to 19.00, but only for trains coming from Leicester. You can shoot trains from both directions well - particularly if you have a telephoto lens and stand about 7-12 feet away from the railway. This applies to videographers as well.
Shots are quite tight from the north side of the crossing, but the line curves just to the east making an interesting telephoto shot.

2) Westbound 170113, from the Crossing's north side.
August, 12:30, dslr@200mm

Washstones Crossing, Frisby on the Wreake

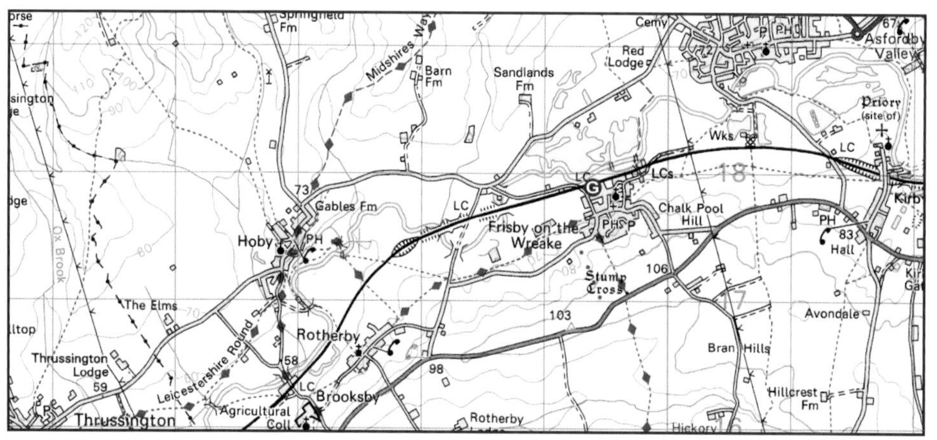

Postcode: LE14 2NR **Lat N52:45:15** **Long W00:58:29**

Road Directions

From M1 travelling north: exit at Junction 21A. From the south: exit at Junction 21, rejoin on the northbound carriageway and exit at Junction 21A. Take the A46 to Wanlip. From here follow signs for East Gosgate. On arrival at East Gosgate take the A607. Keep following this road until you come to the top of a large hill, with a sign - Rotherby. Take the second left after this sign and continue straight down to the bottom of this road until you come to a gate. Open this gate and drive in. Close the gate behind you. Drive towards the railway line. A radio mast makes it easy to spot the location.

You can park on the grass in the field where the crossing is situated.

3) 60029 approaches the crossing with a Peak Forest to Ely working.
Photo by Ben Wheeler, April, 09:45, dslr@48mm

Syston By-Pass Bridge

Location Notes

A busy road overbridge in a short piece of open countryside between Syston and East Goscote.

1) 170398 speeds north with a Cross Country service heading for Stansted Airport.
August, 13:30, dslr@24mm

Public Transport

Arriva services 5/5A operate every 10 minutes from Leicester Bus Station. Service 5, every 20 minutes, operates into the estate at East Goscote, service 5A does not go into the estate but continues along the road to Rearsby.

Amenities

There are none in the immediate area. The nearest shops are in Syston or East Goscote.

Photographic Notes

The line here runs south west to north east, so the sun is on the nose of eastbound trains in the morning until approximately 10.00. Although the sun does not quite get on the nose in the evening, it is possible to get a nice shot of eastbound trains on summer evenings from the north side of the line with the sun pretty much side on to the train. There is no shot from this bridge looking east as it is a totally overgrown tree lined cutting.

Eastbound trains are normally powering here as they are regaining speed after slowing for Syston Junction. Good video zoom sequences can be filmed here but video footage taken from this bridge is likely to suffer with road noise from the busy A607. Southbound workings can be predicted as the signal to the south is usually set to red, protecting Syston Junction beyond. Freight will get a number 3 feather to take the north side of the triangle.

Note: It is possible to chase any train taking the Peterborough line at Syston Junction to this bridge from Cossington, thus enabling two shots to be taken. The road journey takes about three minutes and the rail journey takes about ten minutes.

Syston By-Pass Bridge

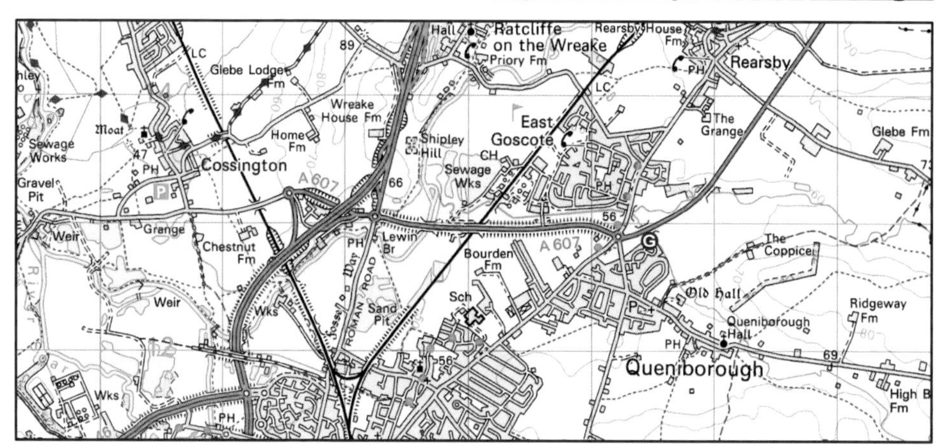

Postcode: LE7 3UL **Lat N52:42:38** **Long W01:04:04**

Road directions

From M1 travelling north: exit at Junction 21A. Travelling south: exit at Junction 21, rejoin on the northbound carriageway and exit at Junction 21A. Take the A46 northwards and turn left just north of Syston (signposted A607). Soon after leaving the A46 there is a roundabout, turn right here and follow the road to the next roundabout where you shouls continue straight on. The road bridge is reached after approximately 800 yards.

Park on the grass verge on the left near to the top of the bridge.

2) 66701 'Whitemoor' powers north with a ballast working to March, Whitemoor yard.
June, 11:45, dslr@65mm

Cossington

Location Notes

In open countryside east of the village of Cossington, these locations are road bridges over the line.

1) 73204/6/9 head north with a 5Z73 Stewarts Lane-Derby move.
Photo by Ben Wheeler, May, 14:30 dslr@55mm.

Public Transport

Kinchbus service 2 operates every 30 minutes between Leicester Bus Station and Loughborough via Sileby. Alight by the pub in Cossington village, walk through the pub car park onto the lane at rear, turn left and follow the lane until it crosses the railway bridge.

Amenities

There are none in the immediate area. The nearest shops, including a chip shop can be found in the centre of Sileby about 1 mile to the north of Cossington. The Thurmaston retail park, about 2 miles away, has some fast food outlets.

Photographic Notes

Southern Bridge(1): Is known to the locals as the 'Commercial Bridge' as it is close to a lorry park called Cossington Commercials. Parking here is limited, but this is the best place to be for a southbound train on the slow line. All trains to or from the Peterborough line at Syston Junction will be on the slow lines at Cossington. The slow lines are the two easternmost tracks.
In summer, the southbound morning shot is good from first light until around 10.00 when the sun comes in line. It is possible to take northbound trains in the morning, but there is a signal in the way. The sun does not get on the front of northbound trains here. After the sun has moved round, it is possible to photograph southbound trains on both the fasts and the slows. It is also possible in high summer to photograph northbound trains from this bridge with the sun on the nose from around 16.00, though you will need a long lens if you do not wish to have signals in your picture.

2) 220220 heads north towards Nottingham.
June, 11:00, dslr@80mm.

Northern Bridge (2): Is known to the locals as Humbles Lane bridge. The morning shot is good for trains on the fast lines but a little tight for trains on the slow lines. The northbound shot gets the sun until around 90 minutes before sunset.
Both bridges are good for video although there is far more risk of traffic noise on the 'Commercial' bridge. It is not possible to do pan shots on either bridge, but long zoom shots are possible. At both locations clearances on the roadside verges are tight so there will be cars and lorries passing very close behind you. This might hinder the use of a a video tripod.

For any train taking the Peterborough line at Syston Junction, it is possible to chase the train to the Syston bypass bridge for a second shot. Head back to the roundabout near the Commercial bridge and then take the A607 towards Melton Mowbray. The road journey takes about three minutes and the rail journey, via the Syston triangle, takes about ten minutes.

Cossington

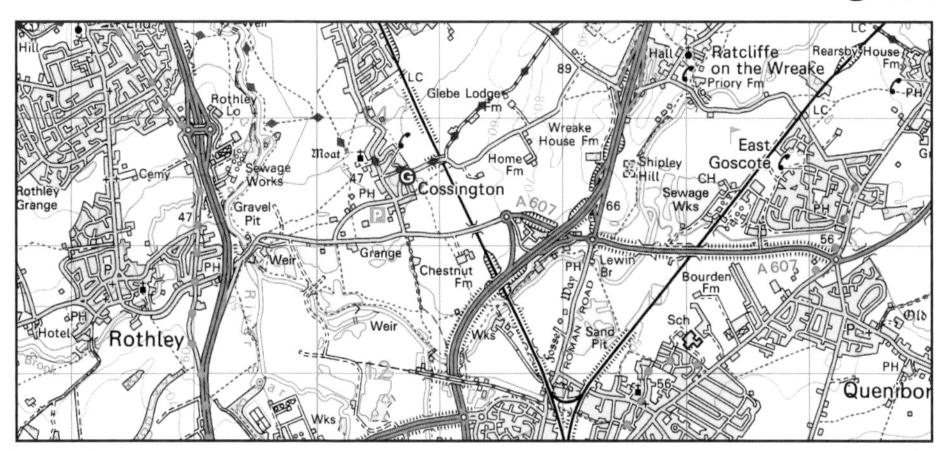

Postcode: LE7 4UT **Lat N52:42:52** **Long W01:05:46**

Road Directions

From M1 travelling north: exit at Junction 21A. From the south: exit at Junction 21, rejoin on the northbound carriageway and exit at Junction 21A. Take the A46 northwards and turn left just north of Syston (signposted A607). Soon after leaving the A46 there is a roundabout, turn left here and the road immediately crosses the railway on an overbridge (location 1). To get to location 2, carry on for approximately 600 yards and turn right into the village of Cossington. Take the first right turn in the village and follow this twisting road until you come to the railway overbridge.

Both locations have roadside verge parking close by.

3) 60044 heads south, on the slow line, with 6m96 Margam to Corby loaded steel coils.
Photo by Ben Wheeler, July, 14:30, dslr@50mm.

Barrow upon Soar

Location Notes

A footbridge joining houses to the east with the riverside area to the south. This footbridge was replaced in 2008 after the original was knocked down by a lorry passing underneath and then hit by 158856 on a Nottingham to Norwich service. The new bridge is a large green metal single arch structure with parapet sides about 5 feet high.

1) GBRf 66718 hauls a Cottam to Hotchley Hill Gypsum working south on the fast line.
August, 14:00, dslr@35mm

Public Transport

There is an hourly train service between Loughborough and Leicester which serves the station at Barrow upon Soar. In addition Kinchbus service 2 operates every 30 minutes between the towns and serves Barrow.

Amenities

There is a good range of shops in Barrow upon Soar.

Photographic Notes

The footbridge, which used to serve the original Barrow upon Soar station, offers shots in both directions. Southbound trains can be photographed with sun on the nose between about 11.00 and 13.30 in the summer. However, trees on the lineside cast shadows which can be problematic.
The northbound shot is ideal for trains on the slow line. Trains on the fast line have to be photographed nearly head on as there is a grey Portacabin and a growth of trees that prevents the photographer from going wide. In the summer, northbound trains have sun on the nose from about 14.30.
The footbridge bridge is good for video as there is no road noise but the bridge does vibrate with passing high speed trains.

Barrow upon Soar

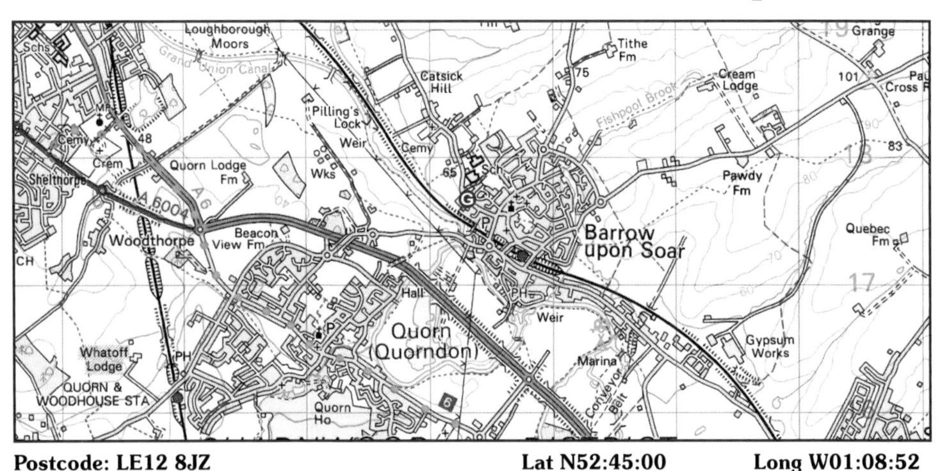

Postcode: LE12 8JZ **Lat N52:45:00** **Long W01:08:52**

Road Directions

From M1 travelling north: exit at Junction 21A. From the south: exit at Junction 21, rejoin on the northbound carriageway and exit at Junction 21A. Take the A46 northwards and after about six miles take the first exit at the roundabout onto the A6. Turn off this road at the north end of Barrow upon Soar (same turning as Quorn). Follow the signs for Barrow, and as you enter the village, drive over the narrow bridge with traffic lights and continue along the road as it climbs up to a roundabout. Take the first exit which goes over the railway line, you will pass a free car park which has a shot of the line through the mesh gates at the end. Continue up the High Street and take the second left onto 'Cotes Road', then take the next left onto 'The Rookeries'. Park here and follow the footpath at the end of the road left to the bridge.

2) 66050 'EWS Energy' heads north, on the slow line. This view shows the 'grey portacabin' and trees on the right.
August, 15:15, dslr@85mm

Kegworth

Location Notes

The location is a road bridge across the line. Traffic is not too heavy but be careful as the pavement on the north side is narrow and there is no pavement at all on the south side of the bridge. As it is only a few miles from East Midlands Airport, aircraft regularly pass overhead just to the south of the bridge.

1) EMT Meridian 222022 heads north with a Derby bound working.
June, 12:00, dslr@24mm

Public Transport

Trent Barton service 'Rainbow 5', from Loughborough to Nottingham, passes over this bridge - there is a stop approximately 50 yards to the West, outside the Railway Inn pub. Catch the bus from either Long Eaton station or Loughborough town centre.
At the time of writing, an all day ticket valid on all Trent Barton services after 09:00 is £4.20. Single/return tickets may be cheaper.

Amenities

There is a pub, the Station Hotel, next to the bridge. Apart from this, the nearest shops are in Kegworth village centre, which has a Co-op etc, and Sutton Bonington.

Accommodation

The Station Hotel, a pub with accommodation, is a few yards away.

Photographic Notes

The line runs roughly north to south. Facing north, the fast lines are on the left. Light is best from mid morning until mid to late afternoon. It is worth standing in the middle of the bridge - in between the fast and slow lines - you can see approximately 2 miles to the north, giving you plenty of time to move if necessary depending where the sun happens to be.
Although the road could not be considered busy, road noise may be a problem for video. Also, aircraft often fly low overhead to the South on the descent to East Midlands Airport.

2) 156404 heads north, away from the camera.
June, 12:00, dslr@24mm

Kegworth

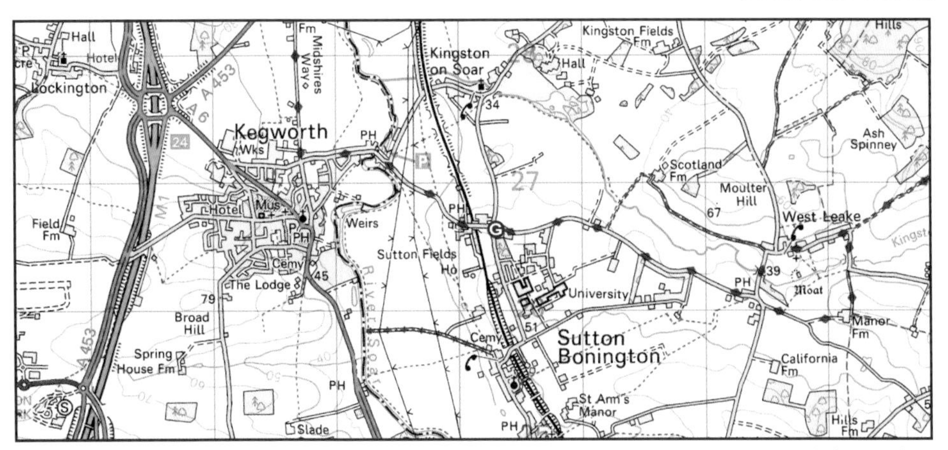

Postcode: LE12 5RJ **Lat N52:50:06** **Long W01:15:27**

Road Directions

From M1 Junction 24: follow the A6 towards Kegworth for about half a mile. Then take the first left, into Side Ley, and keep going for about 1 ¼ miles, towards Sutton Bonington. This will bring you right to the bridge, which is on Station Road.

There are a number of side roads in which you can park a car.

3) Heading north, and away from the camera, an EMT Meridian passes over a track access crossing.
June, 12:00, slr@85mm

East Midlands Parkway

Location Notes

This location is a recently constructed road bridge leading to the new station on the Midland Main Line. The area is mainly open with fields and marinas and no residential areas close by.
A few miles to the north of the location three lines converge from Derby, Sheffield and Nottingham and then all head south towards Leicester. Coal traffic to the power station will not pass this location. The northbound track has been lifted, therefore workings can only enter, or exit, the power station from the other side which is not visible from the location.

1) Testing a refurbished NMT power car a bizarre ensemble of Class 43/31 and MkIIs heads towards Derby.
June, 11:30, dslr@24mm

Public Transport

East Midlands Parkway is served by East Midlands Trains from Derby and Leicester. There is also a park and ride bus service from East Midlands airport if you wish to fly in.

Amenities

The station has basic facilities but little in the way of food and drink. For this you will need to travel to Long Eaton where there are supermarkets and shops.

Photographic Notes

The main shot at this location is one with the cooling towers dominating the skyline. For this you will need a wide angle lens around 20-24mm on a digital SLR. As this shot is facing north it will be well lit from mid morning to quite late in the day. A step ladder is required to see over the top of the bridge sides as they are over 7 feet high, but the ends are just waist high crash barriers.
The approach to the station is in a cutting that slopes down as it goes away from the bridge but should not cause much problem with shadows. The northbound shot is tight and there are far better locations nearby.

East Midlands Parkway

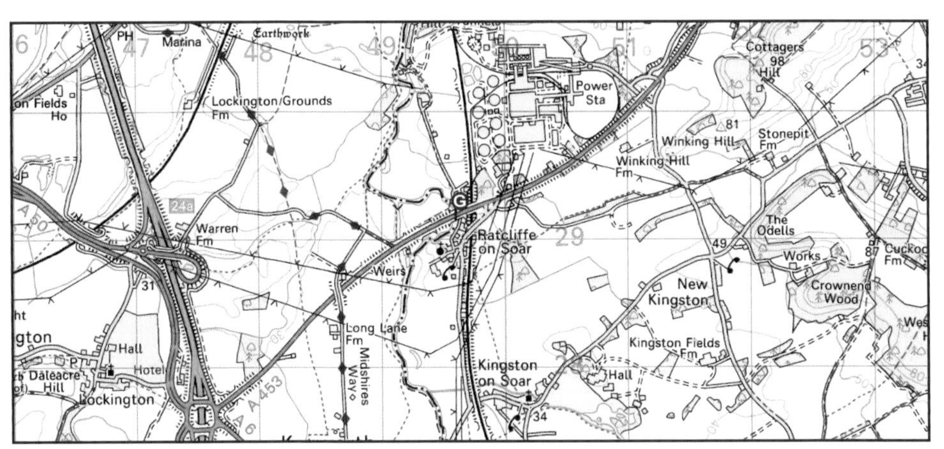

Postcode: NG11 0EE **Lat N52:51:34** **Long W01:15:46**

Road Directions

From M1 Junction 24: take the A453 north east and the station will be signposted. But it is basically along the road and left at the traffic lights.

East Midlands Parkway has a very large car park, or there are a number of building site turn-ins where you could leave a car. But park off the road as a number of buses use this route.

2) Heading away from the camera an EMT 220 speeds north to Nottingham. Taken from the west side of the bridge.
June, 11:15, dslr@24mm

Pride Parkway, Derby

Location notes

An open area next to a wide, busy road that crosses the line. The embankment is quite steep but there is no need to go down it. You can sit on the crash barrier. The road is very wide and as it a busy trunk route through Derby, it is not advisable to cross without taking care.

1) After working up from London, an EMT HST, headed by 43049, slows on the approaches to Derby.
June, 10:15, dslr@28mm

Public transport

Arriva Services 44 and 45 run along London Road, which is the southern end of Pride Parkway. There are also a couple of stops on Pride Parkway itself.

Amenities

There is nothing in the immediate area, but Derby city centre is a short drive/bus ride away.

Accommodation

Derby has plenty of hotels and Bed and Breakfasts. There are also some Travel Inns in the Pride Park.

Photographic notes

The road runs at 90 degrees to the line which is a curve under the bridge, so the light will favour Derby departures up until midday and arrivals after lunch. There are a number of bushes that will start to encroach on the later coaches of workings but nothing on the front few vehicles.
Given the proximity of the A6, road noise will be a serious problem for videographers.

Pride Parkway, Derby

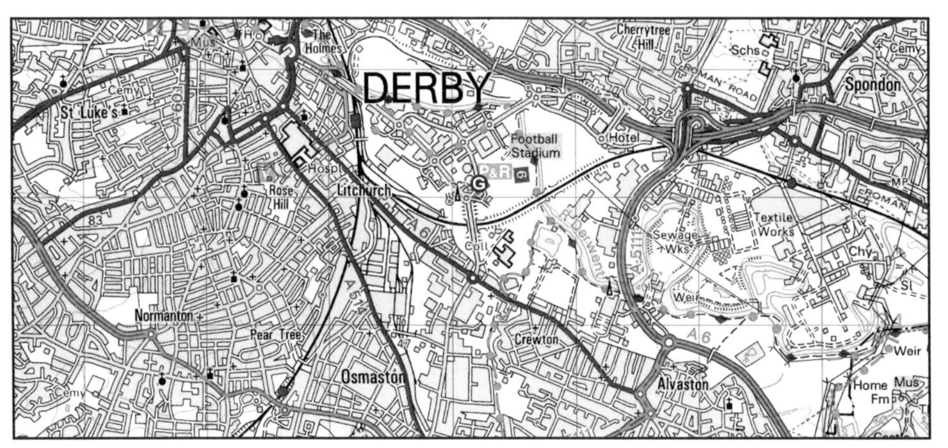

Postcode: DE24 1AJ **Lat N52:54:32** **Long W01:26:56**

Road directions

The location is near the Derby ring road, to the south east of the town centre. Approaching from the A6, take the third exit at the roundabout (Traffic Street) and the third exit at the next roundabout (Station Approach). This will take you over the location.

There is no stopping on the bridge but there is plenty of parking in the retail/industrial units which are only a few minutes walk away.

2) EMT Meridian 222002 departs Derby and heads south towards Leicester and on to London.
June, 10:00, dslr@30mm

Bedford to Leicester

Passenger Traffic

East Midlands Trains operates the passenger service on this section of line. This is in the hands of either class 222 Meridians or HST sets. With services to Derby, Nottingham, Sheffield and Leeds, there will not be long to wait between passenger trains.

1) 222012 arrives at Wellingborough from Mill Road.
June, 12:00, dslr@62mm

Freight Traffic

There is a reasonable amount of freight traffic on the Midland Main line, with operations from both DB Schenker and Freightliner.

There are stone trains from Bardon Hill and cement workings from St Pancras and West Thurrock. But you are unlikely to see anything other than Class 66s on the section south of Wigston Junction in Leicester. North of Wigston junction you will see lots of the cross country intermodal traffic bound for Felixstowe, travelling via Peterborough.

Occasional Traffic

There are often Serco trains heading to the south east of England. The New Measurement Train is timetabled to run on a Thursday.

The GBRf yard at Wellingborough provides a regular, but as required, flow of traffic to work sites around the country. DB Schenker operates 67s and DVTs on the seasonal Rail Head Treatment Trains. There are also frequent unit deliveries from Derby to London and the south east.

2) 37069 takes a Serco back to Derby past Souldrop.
Photo by Richard Tearle, June, 12:00, dslr@24mm

3) 67010 takes a redundant class 309 EMU south from the East Midlands Test Centre line to Shoeburyness for storage.
August, 11:00, dslr@24mm

Bedford to Leicester

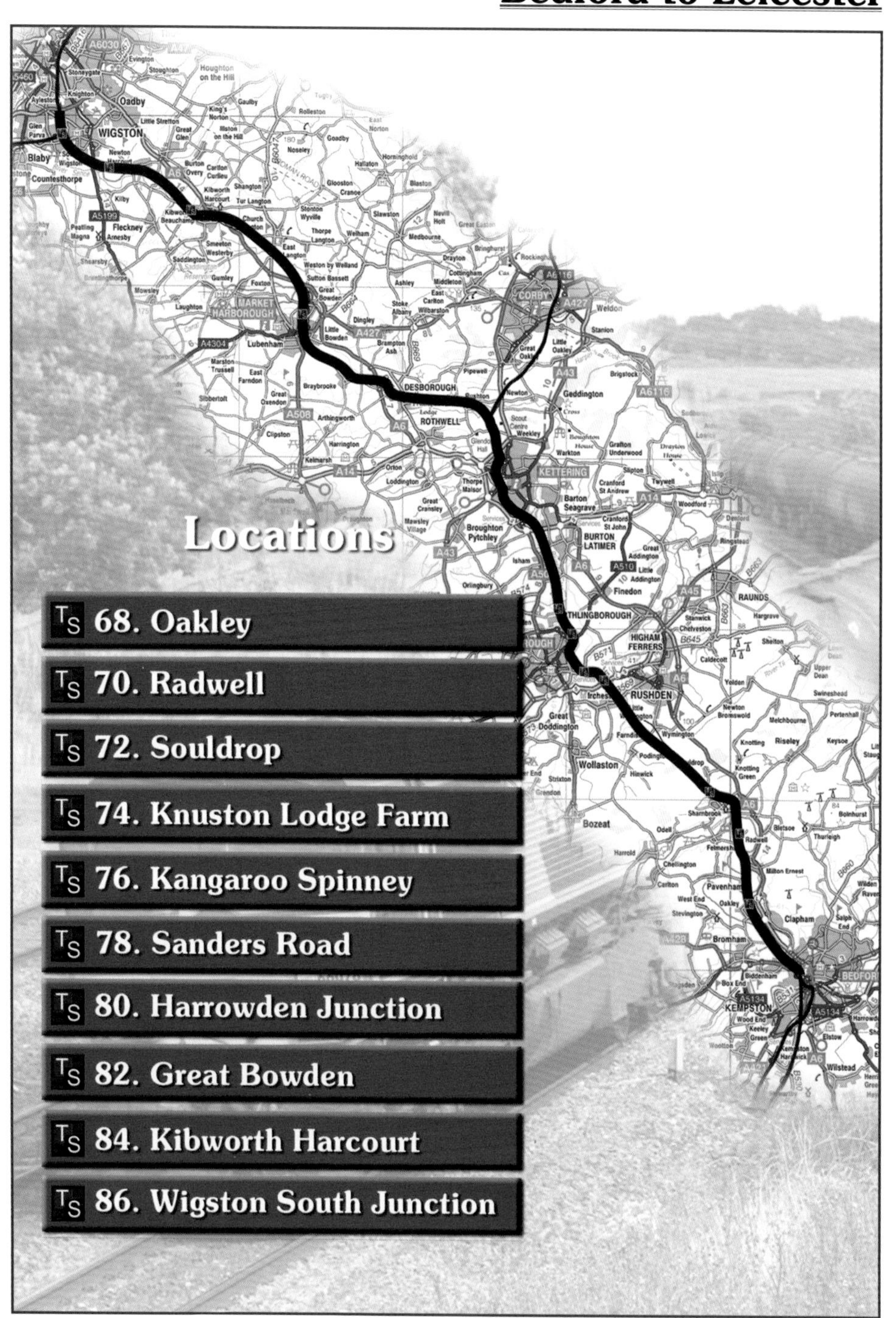

Oakley

Location Notes

Oakley is a small village north of Bedford which had a railway station until it was closed in 1958. The bridge used to lead to the station car park but now ends up at private residences at the end of the road.

1) 50031+49 head south towards Bedford through Oakley with a charter to Alton. Taken from the field to the north.
Photo by Albert Dawson, June, 18:30, slr@28mm

Public Transport

Stagecoach Bedford operate the Route 51 from Bedford to a stop in the village.

Amenities

There is a Sainsbury's superstore just north of Bedford on the A6. Otherwise the nearest amenities would be in Bedford town centre.

Photographic Notes

A very quiet bridge with good views both ways and not much noise to spoil the videos. The bridge sides are low enough to look over but a step ladder might be an advantage.
The northern road bridge, Highfield Road, offers a good, morning view. This bridge is high above the line and shows the sweeping curve. There are also footpaths through the field which offer good morning shots.

2) An EMT Meridian speeds north towards Leicester.
Photo by Albert Dawson, June, 18:30, slr@28mm

Oakley

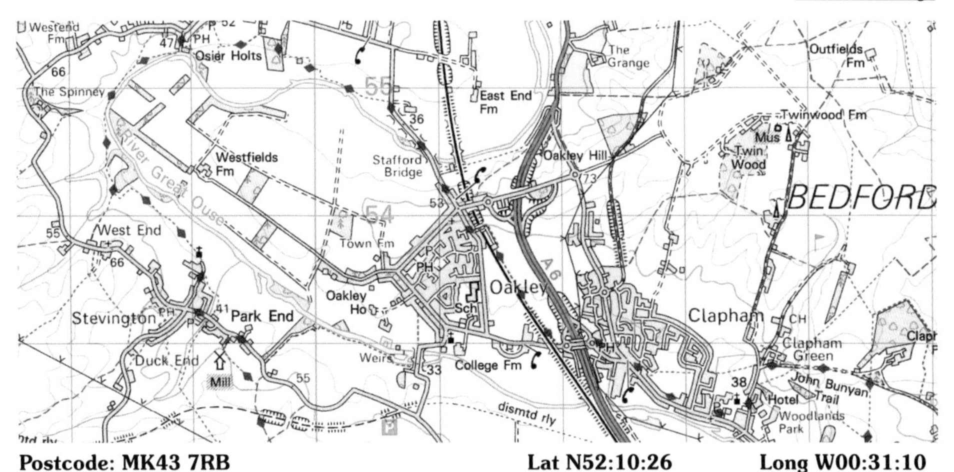

Postcode: MK43 7RB **Lat N52:10:26** **Long W00:31:10**

Road Directions

From the A6 (Paula Radcliffe Way) about 2 miles north of Bedford, take the exit and follow the signs for Oakley. At the crossroads turn left onto Station Road and the turning to the location is the next left.

It is better to park on Station Road than to drive up to the bridge location as, unless you drive to the private residences at the end, there is nowhere to park which will not block the road.

3) 60059 heads north with the Crawley to Peak Forest stone empties.
Photo by John Patston, June, 14:45, slr@85mm

Radwell

Location Notes

The location is around a viaduct in rural Bedfordshire. You are more likely to encounter cows than people. The grassland is a flood plain for the Great Ouse so be prepared to get muddy feet!

1) 43036 leads an East Midlands Trains service south towards Bedford as viewed from near the field entrance.
June, 17:00, dslr@70mm

Public Transport

Stagecoach's 'Mercury M50' service operates hourly between Bedford and Kettering, running along the road between Milton Ernest and Radwell.

Amenities

There is nothing at the location. There is a small village store in Milton Earnest and, on the A6 north of Bedford, there is a Sainsbury's superstore.

Photographic Notes

The location affords decent views of the fast lines in both the up and down directions. But the slow lines are at a higher level and partly shrouded by the viaduct wall (view 4).
Light is best from lunchtime onwards. The shot is best for south facing trains as the viaduct becomes a cutting opposite where you stand and there is no view south. The other option is for a side view across the field (views 1, 2 & 3).

2) A Nottingham to London Meridian crosses the Ouse.
Photo by John Patston, August, 12:12, dslr@50mm

3) On the slow line, 66560 on a Colnbrook to Earles cement working. *Photo by Geoff Plumb, October, 14:20, dslr@xxmm*

Radwell

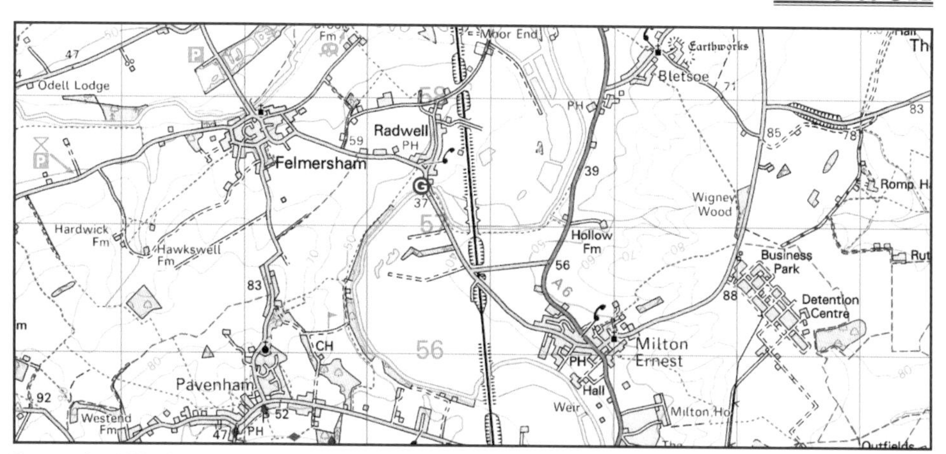

Postcode: MK43 7HU **Lat N52:12:06** **Long W00:31:36**

Road Directions

On the A6 heading north about 4½miles north of Bedford: as you enter the village of Milton Ernest, you will pass some decorative roadside gates. Follow the road as it bends to the left. In the village there is a junction on the left, take this road and follow it out of the village. You will cross the railway and soon after this you will see the viaduct on your right. Should you miss this turning continue through the village and once back into open fields take the next left, follow this road to the end and after crossing the railway turn right and the location is a few hundred yards on the right

There are a few small lay-bys opposite the field. In times of heavy rain this should be just above the water level.

4) 43187 heads south towards Bedford with a Nottingham to London St Pancras service.
Photo by Scott Borthwick, January, 13:30, dslr@54mm

Souldrop

Location Notes

A road bridge surrounded by trees and fields. The bridge has been designated a weak bridge and has been made into a single lane with the provision of extra barriers. This makes the location much safer as there is no need to worry about the cars behind you. At this point the main line is raised and has a steeper gradient over Sharnbrook Summit, whilst the freight line avoids the summit with a gentler climb to the east.

1) 222011 heads north on the main towards Derby.
January, 12:15, dslr@52mm

Public Transport

Both Sharnbrook and Souldrop are reasonably well served by buses from Bedford. The 125 from Bedford to Rushden runs every two hours (first departure 09.00 from Bedford) and drops you in either village. Between Sharnbrook and Souldrop it crosses the railway by one of the bridges featured. The 52 and 53 also serve Sharnbrook (from Bedford) approximately hourly, but this necessitates a 30 minute walk to Souldrop, whilst the 50 from Bedford to Kettering, also hourly from 08.55, runs along the A6, which is only a few hundred yards from either village. All services are run by Stagecoach (United Counties).

2) 66008 northbound on the summit avoiding line.
January, 13:30, dslr@116mm

Amenities

There is a selection of shops in Souldrop village.

Photographic Notes

The embankment offers a good unrestricted view of the side of trains in either direction. The early morning suits southbound shots, with the sun moving to the wrong side of the line after about 11.00. Later in the evening the sun will be better for northbound workings.
The bridge parapet is around 5 feet high so a step ladder will probably not be required to get a view across the top, but the parapet could make setting up all but the tallest video tripods difficult. There is an occasional noise problem with loud engines at the nearby Santa Pod Raceway. This could interfere with sound recording.

Souldrop

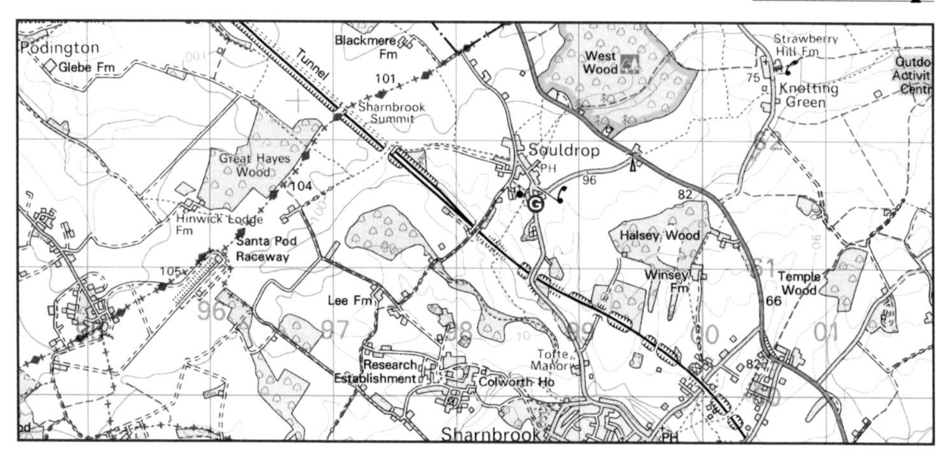

Postcode: MK44 1EX **Lat N52:14:16** **Long W00:33:26**

Road Directions

From the A6 about 3 miles south of Rushedn and about 9 miles north of Bedford, turn west off the road and follow the signs to Sharnbrook, taking the left turn in Souldrop village. When you reach the traffic lights for the bridge you have arrived at the location. You can park on the verges but do not block the work entrances. Alternatively when you see the radio mast on the south side of the A6 take this turn into Souldrop village and follow the road to the location, stopping before the traffic lights.

3) 66103 heads south, with an engineers track working, on the freight line towards Bedford.
Photo by Richard Tearle, August, 09:30, slr@85mm

Knuston Lodge Farm

Location Notes

This is a bridge, field and riverside location on the A45. The road bridge has very heavy, fast traffic passing behind you. The pavement on which you stand is very wide, so it is not dangerous but the lorries can produce some turbulence. The field and riverside positions offer views of the 13 arch viaduct spanning the river Nene.

1) 222002 speeds north, away from the camera.
June, 10:45, dslr@50mm

Public Transport

The nearest bus service is X46 which operates every 30 minutes between Northampton, Wellingborough and Irchester. The bus stops in the village from where it is a 15-20 minute walk to the bridge.

2) 66117 heads north into Wellingborough with Bletchley-Peak Forest stone empties.
June, 10:45, dslr@85mm

Amenities

There are no amenities in the immediate area. There are a few petrol stations dotted along the A45. Apart from those, Wellingborough town has a range. of shops, cafes and pubs.

Photographic Notes

Good views of the line sweeping through countryside over the viaduct can be had here with the Sharnbrook summit avoiding line on the higher level of the two. There is no real opportunity to photograph approaching northbound workings from the bridge as the very busy dual carriage way (A45) would have to be crossed but there is plenty of notice of southbound workings.

3) A southbound Meridian crosses the river Nene viaduct.
June, 11:15, dslr@85mm

Other views of the viaduct are available from the fields by following the path down from the main parking spot. This path runs down to the river then either under the viaduct to the right, or to a river crossing on the left. The shot from the other side of the viaduct is only really suited to early morning workings on the slow lines.

Knuston Lodge Farm

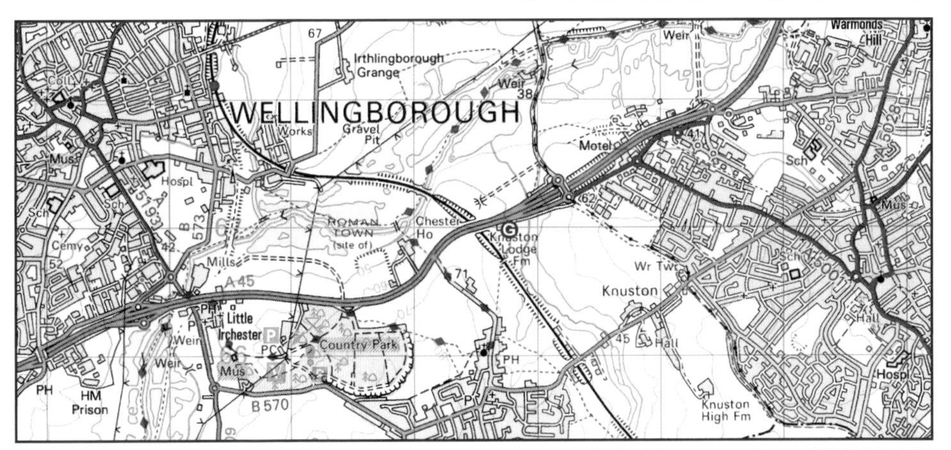

Postcode: NN29 7HB **Lat N52:17:37** **Long W00:38:44**

Road Directions

The location is on the A45, about a mile to the west of Rushden and two miles to the east of Wellingborough,on the eastbound carriage way, There is a lay-by with a turning into a field just before the green exit sign for junction 16 - Rushden and Irchester. Park in, but do not obstruct, this field gateway.

If you are travelling from the Rushden direction, turn round at junction 16 and continue back along the A45 to the lay-by.

4) 31459 top and tails with 31106 on a Derby to Selhurst Serco test train movement. Seen from the bank of the Nene.
Picture by Peter Foster, February, 12:00, dslr@26mm

Kangaroo Spinney

Location Notes

A very narrow road overbridge with a tight road approach bend. Traffic will be travelling slowly but there are often large lorries coming in and out of the Leyland Industrial Estate.

1) Retaining it's former Midland Main Line colours EMT 222018 heads south after departing Wellingborough Station.
Photo by Jason Rodhouse, June, 12:15, dslr@70mm

Public Transport

The bridge is about a 10 minute walk from Wellingborough Station.

Amenities

There is a cafe in the Leyland industrial estate that is open 07.30 to 14.00 Monday to Fridays, otherwise Wellingborough has a wide range of shops.

2) 66184 on a cement train, from further down the path, using steps.
Photo by Jason Rodhouse, February, 14:00, dslr@52mm

Photographic Notes

This is the best location for northbound afternoon shots in the area. You will have to climb over a low crash barrier at the side of the road to get to the shot position. There is room to set up a video tripod if required but noise from the road would interfere with audio recordings.
A southbound shot is also possible from the other side of the road but you are standing with your back to the road on a very tight corner so it would be better to shoot somewhere else if you are after a number of southbound workings.

Kangaroo Spinney

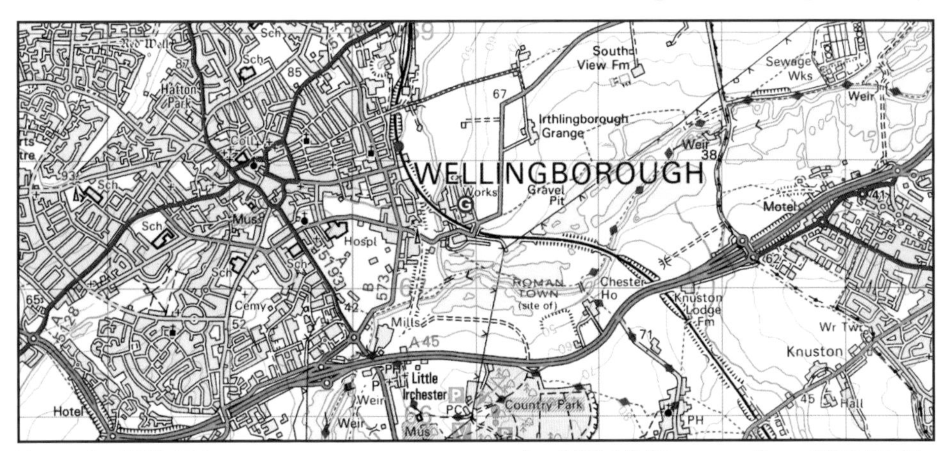

Postcode: NN8 1RS **Lat N52:17:52** **Long W00:40:03**

Road Directions

On the A6 at Irthlingborough, about 16 miles north of Bedford, take the first exit at the roundabout (Station Road) and enter the town. Take the second exit at the next roundabout onto the B571 and continue towards Wellingborough. As you enter Wellingborough the road crosses the railway and turns sharply right. The location is over the crash barrier on this curve.

You can park either in the Industrial Estate located before crossing the railway or opposite the derelict land after the bridge.

3) Unusually on the fast lines 66078 heads an oil working north.
Photo by Jason Rodhouse, July, 14:00, dslr@70mm

Sanders Road

Location Notes

A footbridge located down the side of the Weatherbys factory on Sanders Road, Wellingborough.

1) 66164 heads north with La Farge empties for Mountsorrel. Unusually, for freight, this working is on the main line.
Photo by Mark Bearton, April, 09:15, dslr@70mm

Public Transport

The bridge is about a mile and a half from Wellingborough station and as it is near an industrial estate there is little in the way of public transport.

Amenities

There are usually a few 'burger vans' on the factory estate, and Wellingborough town centre has a range of of shops and take aways.

Photographic Notes

The southbound shot is best in the morning, the northbound shot from mid afternoon. However the rubbish often strewn along the fence from the Council tip does not make the eastern side of the northbound shot a very pleasant picture.

2) 66731 heads north with a 377 unit move to Derby.
Photo by Mark Bearton, April, 13:15, dslr@100mm

Sanders Road

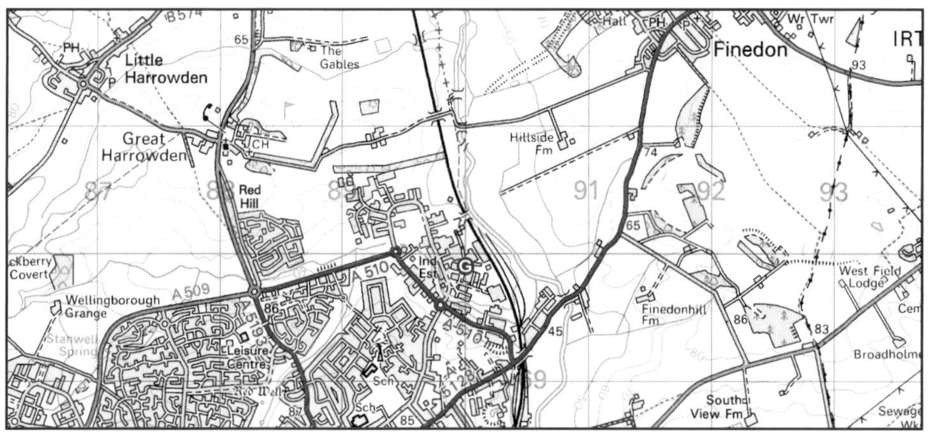

Postcode: NN8 4BX **Lat N52:19:24** **Long W00:40:52**

Road Directions

On the A6 at Irthlingborough, about 16 miles north of Bedford, take the first exit at the roundabout (Station Road) and enter the town. Take the second exit at the next roundabout onto the B571 and continue towards Wellingborough. After about 2 miles turn right into Sidegate Lane and then turn left onto the A510 (Wellingborough Road). Continue on this road, turnining right after crossing the railway. Take the third exit at the next roundabout. and follow the road round to the Weatherbys factory. The lane is after Weatherbys. Park in the roadway between the Weatherbys site and the storage depot next to it. Do not attempt to take a car more than about 50 yards down this road. Walk down the road past a caravan parked on the road and pick your way carefully through the debris that accompanies the gypsy site.

3) 222009 slows on the approach to Wellingborough station with a London bound service.
Photo by Mark Bearton, April, 13:15, dslr@85mm

Harrowden Junction

Location Notes

A narrow but busy open bridge with low parapet sides, situated between Harrowden and Finedon.

1) 66150 heads south with an engineers working to Forders.
Photo by Jason Rodhouse, May, 08:15, dslr@39mm

This is the point where freight used to rejoin the main line from the line avoiding Sharnbrook Summit. Although the junction still exists and is used, the freight line has been extended recently to continue north of this location right through to Glendon Junction where the Corby line diverges.

Public Transport

Due to its rural nature, there is no practical public transport to this location. Wellingborough Station is about 3 miles away.

Amenities

The nearest amenities are in Wellingborough.

Photographic Notes

This is a southbound shot throughout the day but only a northbound shot from mid afternoon. Given the open nature of the location, aside from the bridge, there is nothing to cast shadows over your subject matter.
Line speed is 100mph on the main with 50mph on the freight avoider, but freights will be moving slower if taking the junction to cross to the main lines. You can see for a mile or two to the north so there is plenty of notice of approaching workings. The view to the south is not as far, as the line disappears under a bridge round the curve but you will still get ample notice of approaching workings.

2) 43074 heads into Wellingborough.
June, 13:30, dslr@48mm

3) Bound for Mountsorrel 66044 heads north.
Photo by Jason Rodhouse, May, 09:00, dslr@70mm

Harrowden Junction

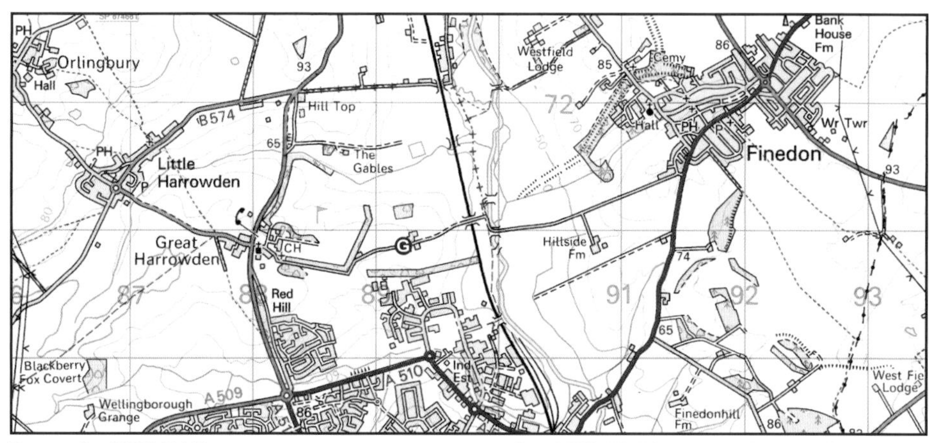

Postcode: NN9 5AE **Lat N52:19:52** **Long W00:41:09**

Road Directions

From the A6 about 5 miles south of Kettering, take the A510 through Finedon. At the edge of the village turn right onto Harrowden Lane, which will lead you to the location.

From Wellingborough: Take the A509 towards Kettering. Turn right just before the speed camera into 'The Slips'. Follow the winding 'Harrowden Lane' to the railway - about a mile.

There are a number of lay-bys and grass verges around the bridge where you can park.

4) 66522 crosses the junction ladder with northbound Bardon stone working of empty hoppers.
June, 12:45, dslr@72mm

Great Bowden

Location Notes

The village of Great Bowden is a suburb of Market Harborough. The location is a footbridge on the outskirts of the village with a park on one side, and fields on the other. The footbridge is of an arched latticed design and will not require a step ladder.

1) 222023 speeds north with a Leicester bound EMT working.
June, 14:30 dslr@24mm

Public Transport

Woods Coaches service 33 offers an hourly service from the Market Harborough Market Hall to Great Bowden, except on Sundays. From the station, on the car park side, walk up Great Bowden Road for about a mile and a half to reach the location.

2) Passing EMT Meridians are framed by the bridge iron work.
June, 14:45 dslr@24mm

Amenities

The park has public toilets open from 08.00 to 19.00 (summer) or 16.30 (winter). The village has two handy shops: Bowden Stores, and Weltons, the latter also serves tea, and coffee and on hot days, home made ice cream. There are also some pubs within walking distance.

Photographic Notes

Shots can be had from both sides of the footbridge. However, the line runs north to south here, so the location is best for southbound workings, preferably in the afternoon.

Great Bowden

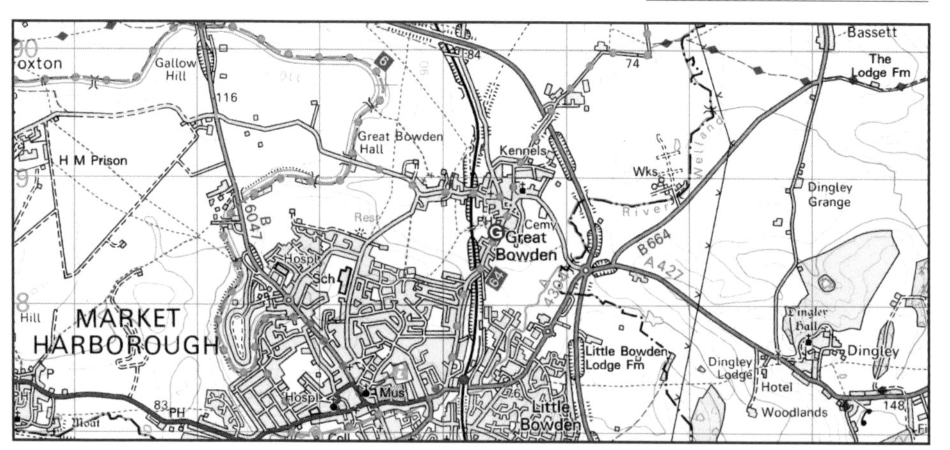

Postcode: LE16 7HX **Lat N52:29:26** **Long W00:54:30**

Road Directions

From the A6: at the A6/A427/A4304 roundabout on the A6 at Market Harborough, take the second exit (Dingley Road). Follow this to Great Bowden and take Station Road southwards. After passsing Horse Shoe lane on your left, look for some signs on the right pointing the way to 'Recycling Bank' and 'Tennis Club'. Take this footpath to the footbridge.

The park has a car park that is open from 08.00 to 19.00 (summer) or 16.30 (winter). If this is closed then park considerately at the roadside.

3) Heading the southbound leg of Spitfire Tours 'Rutland Renegade' 20306/309/314 head south.
Photo by Richard Tearle, August, 12:30, slr@34mm

Kibworth Harcourt

Location Notes

The location is an overbridge in the countryside, between Leicester and Market Harborough. The road here can be quite busy at times but the roadside verges are quite wide.

1) 66623 heads south with a FLHH aggregates working.
Photo by Jason Rodhouse, March, 13:30, dslr@55mm

Public Transport

Stagecoach X3 and 131 services run along the A6 through Kibworth Harcourt village between Market Harborough Square and Leicester, St. Maragrets Bus Station. It would then be a 10-15 minute walk through the village, then down Wistow Road to the location.

Amenities

There is nothing at the location. But Kibworth Village has shops and a post office.

Photographic Notes

Good shots can be obtained from both sides of the bridge here. If the light is good, shots of southbound workings can be had until the early afternoon after which the sun becomes right for the northbound workings. The hill side on the left of the northbound shot has a housing development on it, at the time of writing no houses had been built but the shot background will change over the next few years.

Road noise may make this location unsuitable for video, but it would only be vehicles passing at the wrong moment rather than a constant drone of passing traffic.

Shots can be had at the other bridge to the east, but the trees are quite tall and shadows can be troublesome. However, if it is overcast, it may be worth trying there for a little variety.

Kibworth Harcourt

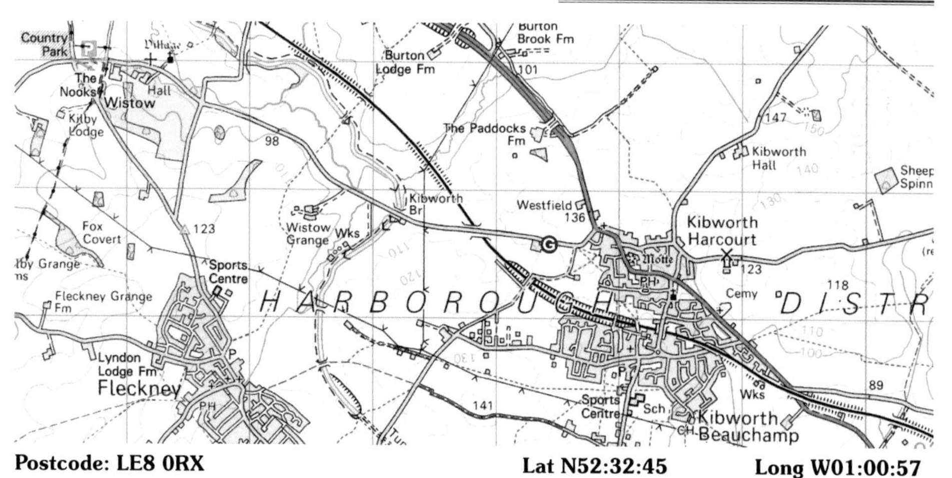

Postcode: LE8 0RX **Lat N52:32:45** **Long W01:00:57**

Road Directions

Kibworth Harcourt is a village on the A6 about 9 miles north of Market Harborough. As you near the north end of the village (there will be a church to the east) turn towards Wistow. Keep on this road until you reach the railway bridge.

Park on the grass verges here, but take care when doing so. There are also some large field entrances further along the lane, these should be suitable if you take care not to block them.

2) 66717 heads north towards Leicester with a 'slinger'.
Photo by Jason Rodhouse, March, 14:30 dslr@75mm

Wigston South Junction

Location Notes

A road bridge that overlooks Wigston South Junction at the site of the former Wigston Magna station.

1) 220016 heads south, out of Leicester with an East Midlands Trains working to London St Pancras.
June, 08:45, dlr@200mm

Public Transport

The nearest station is South Wigston which is served by hourly trains between Leicester, Nuneaton and Birmingham and is a 5-10 minute walk away.
Arriva services 47/48 operate a circular route every 15 minutes in each direction which crosses the bridge. From Leicester the 47 is slightly quicker.

Amenities

There are plenty of shops in the centre of Wigston about 400 yards from the bridge, as well as a Tesco superstore a few minutes to the west. There is also a small newsagents shop to the left of the mini roundabout on the east side of the overbridge, about 50 yards from the bridge.

2) 222018 approaches Leicester.
June, 08:30, dslr@85mm

Photographic Notes

Southbound shots are best in the morning until about 10.30 from the east side of the bridge. It is possible to shoot trains on the up fast, bi-directional slow (the third track across - most likely for a southbound freight) and trains coming off the Wigston curve.
In the evening the sun will be on the nose of northbound trains and it is possible to photograph any train that uses the down fast. It should also be noted that any freight booked to go round Wigston curve will use this track, together with any northbound freights that need to be looped.
The location is interesting for video in both directions though you will have to compete with the road noise. Southbound workings normally apply power as they come off Wigston North Junction but northbound trains are normally coasting as they slow down for the Leicester stop.

3) 66614 takes the slow lines south.
June, 08:30, dslr@85mm

Wigston South Junction

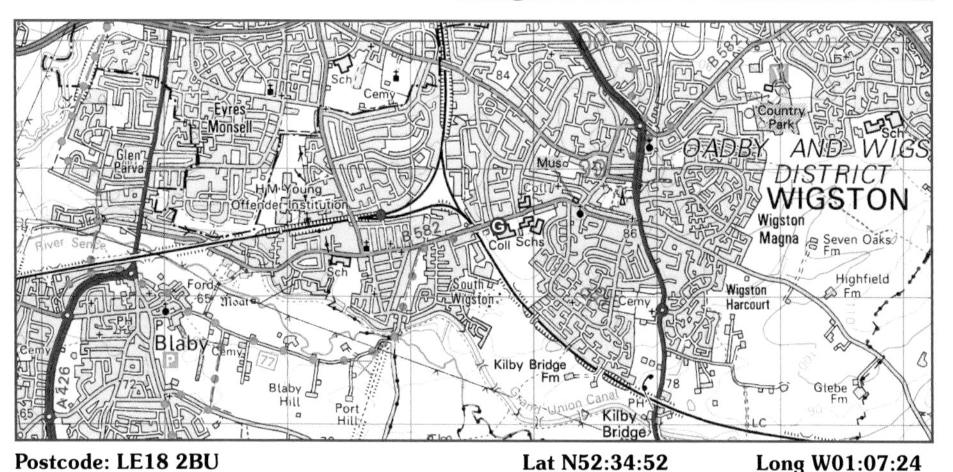

Postcode: LE18 2BU **Lat N52:34:52** **Long W01:07:24**

Road Directions

From M1 Junction 21: take the Leicester outer ring road (A563) towards Oadby. Follow this road until you reach the 'Pork Pie Island' (it has a library situated on it which looks like a pork pie!). At this roundabout turn right towards South Wigston and follow this road right to the end (about 1½ miles). At the end of this road there is a mini roundabout, turn left here into the centre of Wigston. Follow this road through the centre of Wigston for about 1 mile and you will come to the overbridge.

There is limited parking in side streets on the opposite side of the bridge.

4) 43049, in the New East Midlands Trains colours, heads a London bound working away from Leicester.
June, 08:30, dslr@24mm

Bedford to Bletchley

Passenger Traffic

This line is firmly in the hands of London Midland 150s or 153s. Two units usually operate the service.

1) In Sliverlink colours, 150121 operates the line's shuttle, seen here at Lidlington.
Photo by Richard Tearle, August. 10:15, slr@200mm

Freight Traffic

The Bletchley to Peak Forest stone working, seen in many of the images in this chapter, no longer runs so there is no scheduled freight traffic currently using this line.

2) 60059 with Peak Forest stone empties heads east.
Photo by Richard Tearle, January, 11:30, slr@50mm

Occasional Traffic

The line is frequently used for special workings heading down the Midland Main Line.
Most workings will use this line to gain access to the south or west of England. Although there is a freight line from Cricklewood, through Dudding Hill, to Kew, in London, that allows traffic to get to the Southern Region, these are very slow lines that are not available during some parts of the day.
Traffic usually takes this line and then joins the West Coast Main Line to access places like Acton, for the Great Western, or Kensington Olympia, for the Southern Region.
Unit moves from Derby Litchurch Lane to the southern region will also often take this route.
There is no access from London on the Midland Main line or from the north from the West Coast Main Line.

3) 67006 westbound on the Northern Belle, Lidlington.
July, 10:30, dslr@50mm

Bedford to Bletchley

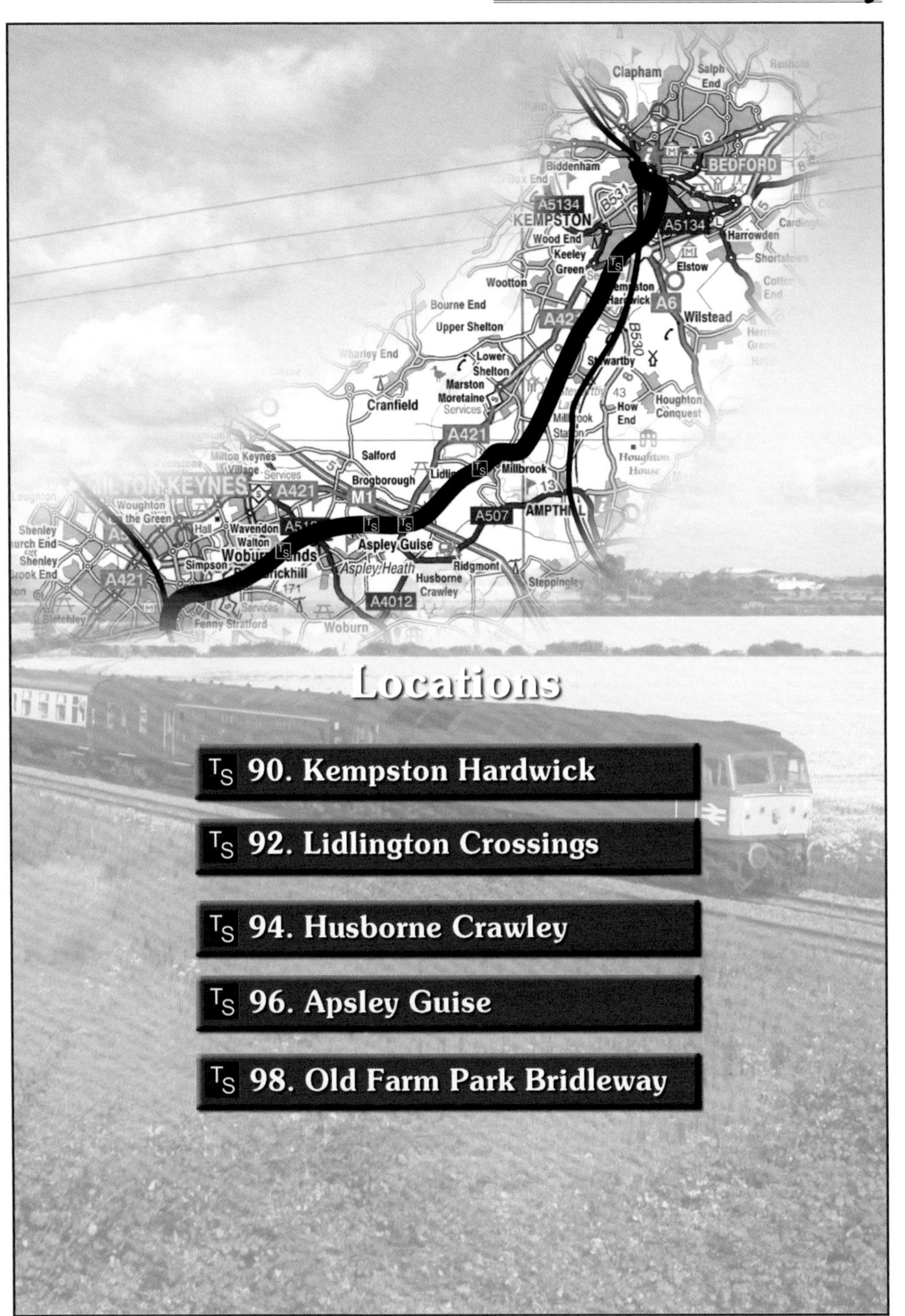

Kempston Hardwick

Location Notes

A rural location on the outskirts of Bedford. The location is a bridge carrying the busy A421 over the railway, or a foot crossing between industrial units and open fields to the south of Bedford.
At the time of writing the location is subject to road works as the A421 is being upgraded to dual carriageway through to the M1. This work is due to finish late in 2010. It is expected that the bridge will eventually be widened or replaced. This should not have a substantial effect on the shot of northbound workings although you might end up with a slightly different view.

1) 150102 heads past the foot crossing north towards Bedford.
August, 10:30, slr@50mm

Public Transport

The nearest bus services to this location are Stagecoach's services 1 and 2 from Bedford to Hastings Road in Kempston, which run every six minutes.
You will then need to walk along Harter Road onto Woburn Road (the A5134) then south to the roundabout where it meets the A421, then along the A421 to the bridge. This walk would take about 15 minutes.
Alternatively there are buses from the Railway Station to the Kempston Interchange Retail Park. The walk from there would be about 10 minutes.

Amenities

You will often find 'burger van' type amenities in the Woburn Road industrial estate opposite the foot crossing. The Interchange Retail Park, about 5 minutes walk to the east, has a McDonald's and Burger King. In addition, the town of Bedford is close by, with plenty of shops and food outlets. The Asda buildings in the distance are a distribution centre, not a superstore.

Accommodation

Bedford offers a variety of places to stay, there is a Travelodge near the junction of the A6/A421. Some local farms, situated along the A421, also do Bed and Breakfast.

2) 150102 passes the radio mast opposite the location.
August, 10:30, slr@48mm

Photographic Notes

This line runs north to south so each end of the day is best, assuming the sun appears. The favoured shot from the bridge is of northbound traffic heading to Bedford which is well lit up to mid morning. From the bridge the southbound shot is hindered by trees. From the foot crossing there are north and southbound shots, if shooting a wide southbound shot there is a radio mast that some may object to.
The A6 is a busy road, videos from the bridge would be very noisy. The foot crossing would be quieter.

Kempston Hardwick

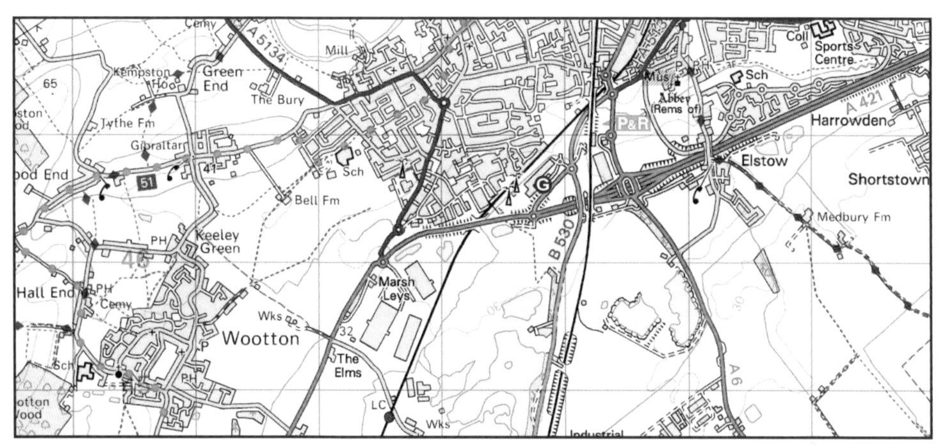

Postcode: MK42 7AZ **Lat N52:06:19** **Long W00:29:38**

Road Directions

From M1 Junction 13: take the A421, signposted for Marston Moretaine. The Bedford to Bletchley line will be on your right along this road. After passing over the bridge location and just before the junction with the A6 is the turning into the Interchange Retail Park. Turn into the retail park, park your car and walk back to the location. Alternatively you can go into the Woburn Road Industrial Park and follow Wolseley Road through the park. At the end of this road, it has become Chantry Road after the right hand bend, park and follow the footpath round the warehouses to the foot crossing.

3) 37609 and 611 top and tail a Milton Keynes to Derby, via Bletchley, Serco Track Recording Test Train.
August, 10:45, dslr@120mm

Lidlington Crossings

Location Notes

Lidlington is located between the stations of Ridgmont and Millbrook. The foot crossings are little used. The footpath is well used by dog walkers, but they rarely cross the line.

1) Taken from the footpath up the hill from crossing No.4, 60002 heads an Peak Forest stone working towards Bedford.
Photo by Richard Tearle, August, 10:45, slr@100mm

Public Transport

Lidlington station is served by hourly trains from Bedford and Bletchley and, depending on the crossing, can be a 15 minute walk away.

Amenities

There are a few local shops and pubs on the High Street/Marsdon Road which is five minutes walk from the station and crossings

Photographic Notes

The four crossings offer a variety of heights relative to the track. Some have steps down to track level and some with steps up embankments. All are on a straight section of track and favour east bound traffic until mid morning. After that the sun is suitable for westbound traffic.
The footpath continues up the hill, south from crossing four. From here you can get wide, side shots (view 1).

2) No.2 - 60067 with stone empties heads to Bedford.
Photo by Richard Tearle, August, 10:45, slr@35mm

3) No.1 - 60100 heads west over Bye Road crossing.
Photo by Richard Tearle, February, 10:45, slr@50mm

Lidlington Crossings

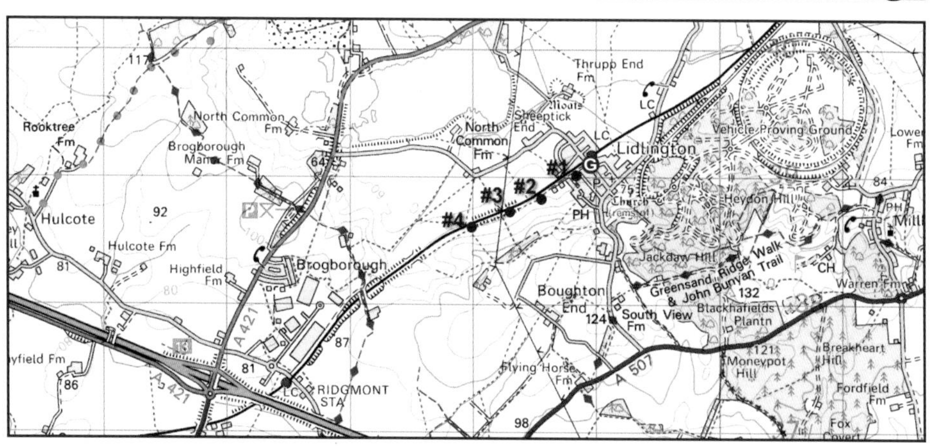

Postcode: MK43 0SA **Lat N52:02:13** **Long W00:34:26**

Road Directions

From M1 Junction 13: follow the A421 towards Bedford. Just after the village of Bogborough is an exit on the right hand side of the road signposted Lidlington. Follow this road. You can either park in a lay-by on this road and follow the respective footpaths south to the crossings or you can carry on until you come to the level crossing at the station. The best parking is just past this on Bye Road. If you miss this turning the next turning on the right also leads to Lidlington.

From here you can follow the footpath, which runs parallel with the line, to the crossings.

4) From crossing No.3, XP64 repaint 47853 heads towards Bedford with a charter.
Photo by Richard Tearle, July, 09:15, slr@85mm

A507 Bridge, Husborne Crawley

Location Notes

Husborne Crawley is located between the stations of Aspley Guise and Ridgmont, quite near M1 Junction 13. The location is the road side of the A507, and although there are a number of trees, there are plenty of wide spaces to shoot through. There is no shelter should the weather turn nasty but the parking space is quite close.

1) 60071 takes the Peak Forest Stone empties east towards Bedford.
Photo by Richard Tearle, August, 10:30, slr@160mm

Public Transport

The nearest station to the bridge is Ridgmont which has hourly trains from Bedford and Bletchley.

Amenities

The truck stop behind you often has burger vans and snack bars and there are toilet facilities on the site.

2) The standard for passenger traffic, 150123, heads to Bedford.
Photo by Albert Dawson, July, 08:45, dslr@100mm

Photographic Notes

The line is quite straight here and very open. This is a west facing, morning only shot. As this is the only bridge over this line that favours this direction it can be a popular location.
There are shots from both the north and south sides of the bridge.
The east facing shot, although on a nice curve, is marred by tall line side vegetation.
The bridge is on a busy road, with HGV services on the other side of the road, consequently there are lots of lorries and it can be quite noisy at times.

A507 Bridge, Husborne Crawley

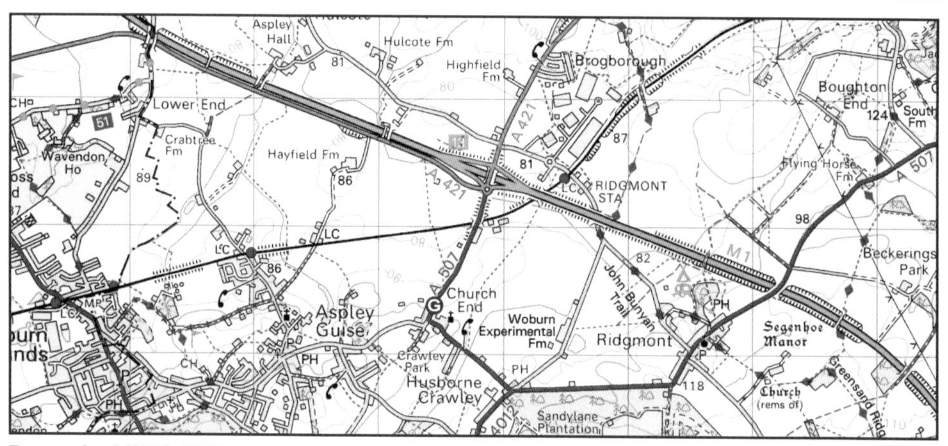

Postcode: MK43 0UT **Lat N52:01:21** **Long W00:36:23**

Road Directions

From M1 Junction 13: exit and head south on the A507. Just before the bridge over the railway on the left is a small parking space. The location is on the other side of the road, on the bank down towards the line. On the M1 side of the bridge is an old field entrance with plenty of space for several cars. (NB: if you are there first, try to park all the way down at the bottom.)

Do not park in what looks like a lay-by - it is what the HGV's use to make wide turns out of the services. Either traffic police will make you move on when, not if, they pass by and see you parked there, or a HGV will clip your car. The owners of the garage will also be swift to move you on if you park in their area.

3) XP64 repaint 47853 heads towards Bedford with a charter from Guildford to Nottingham.
Photo by Albert Dawson, July, 09:00, dslr@28mm

Aspley Guise, Berry Lane Crossing

Location Notes

Aspley Guise crossing is situated between the stations of Aspley Guise and Ridgmont, at the end of Berry Lane which serves several houses.
This is a small road crossing with manually operated gates. There are several houses on the other side of the lane but the lane is quite quiet. There is no shelter should the weather turn nasty.

2) With a Serco Test Train bound for the Bletchley Flyover, 37606 heads west. Taken from the fence.
August, 08:15, slr@24mm

Public Transport

By far the easiest way to this location is to use the rail service from either Bletchley or Bedford. There are several infrequent buses, all originating at Leighton Buzzard, including services 10 and 139 operated by Palmer and Lichfield respectively. From the station, walk south down Salford Road until you come to the entrance to Berry Lane on the right, follow this road until you come to the crossing. This should be a 15 to 20 minute walk.

Amenities

There are no amenities in the immediate area but there is a public house and the usual range of village shops in Aspley Guise.

Photographic Notes

The line runs mainly east to west but slightly south east to north west at this point. Photography is best in the morning for eastbound traffic, and best in the afternoon for westbound traffic. The line is very straight in both directions, bordered by trees, making shot angles quite head on but you can use the fences and gates, carefully, to gain some height.
A shot from the north side of the line is possible, although you are on a private road, so permission should be sort.

Aspley Guise, Berry Lane Crossing

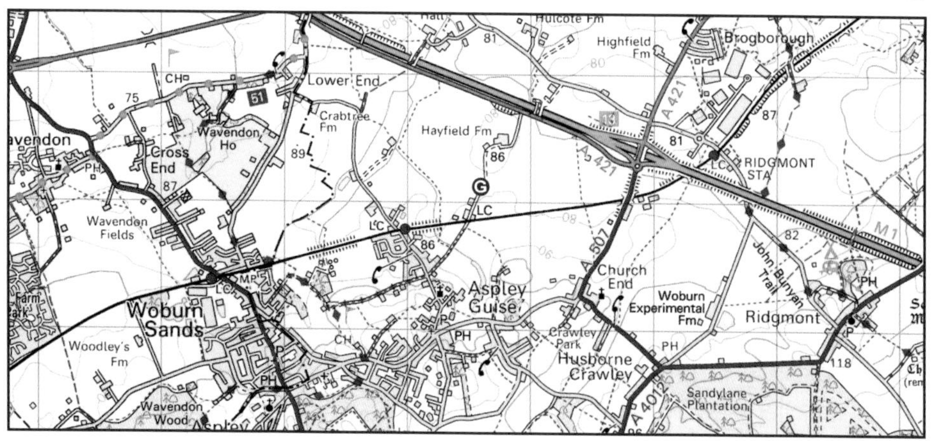

Postcode: MK17 8HS **Lat N52:01:19** **Long W00:37:28**

Road Directions

From M1 Junction 13: exit and head south on the A507. Continue on this road (ignoring the popular turn to Leighton Buzzard and Bedford), into the village of Aspley Guise. Take the first road on the right, called Church Street, the turning is recognisable by a small wooden band stand structure. Follow this road then take the next right, down Berry Lane.

There is a small amount of parking to the south of the crossing. Please note that the road to the north of the crossing is a private road. Make sure you leave enough room for the gates to be opened and for passing traffic to get past.

2) 60086, heading east, with the empty stone turn from Bletchley to Peak Forest approaches the crossing.
Photo by Richard Tearle, July, 10:30, slr@70mm

Old Farm Park Bridleway

Location Notes

Old Farm Park bridleway is located between the stations of Bow Brickhill and Woburn Sands, on the southern outskirts of Milton Keynes. It is a small bridleway with modern gates across the line.

1) London Midland 153371 heads towards Woburn then on to Bedford.
August, 08:45, dslr@52mm

This location is on the very southern outskirts of Milton Keynes, with most of the housing and light industry hidden behind trees to the north and with tree lined fields to the south. There is a tarmac path right up to the gates which extends several feet on the southern part of the line.
Few people use the crossing, even the local dog walkers usually turn back at the gates. There is nowhere to shelter should the weather turn nasty. Old Farm Park is one of the nicer parts of Milton Keynes.

Public Transport

The nearest station is Woburn Sands which is served by hourly trains from Bedford and Bletchley. This walk will take about 25 minutes.
MK Metro service 8 operates every 30 minutes from Milton Keynes station to Bletchley via Bittern Grove in Old Farm Park. You can then walk via Bittern Grove to access the footpath. Note: you need the service 8 that goes to Bletchley, other services to Woburn Sands do not serve Old Farm Park.

Amenities

There is a local shopping centre in Old Farm Park, along Britten Grove, which includes a Tesco Metro. There are many shops in the centre of Milton Keynes and both Bletchley and Milton Keynes stations have several shops.

Photographic Notes

The Bedford to Bletchley line runs mainly east to west but slightly south east to north west at this point. Photography is best in the morning for eastbound traffic and in the afternoon for westbound traffic. The trees to the north can make a nice backdrop but the trees to the south block the weak winter light - so this location is better in the summer months. The line is very straight here towards the east with a sharp curve to the west.
Standing behind the gate to the south of the line affords views in either direction but you are slightly below the line, which suits some people's style of photography. Others may wish to either bring a step ladder or balance carefully on the gates.

Old Farm Park Bridleway

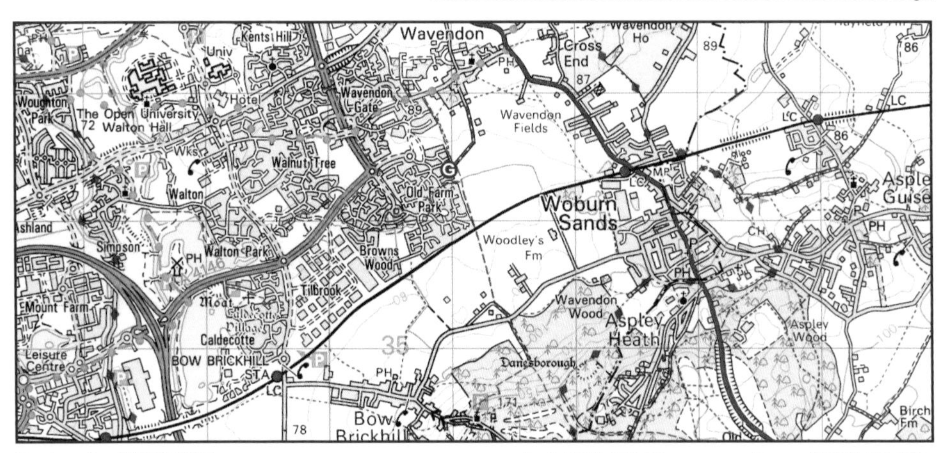

Postcode: MK7 8RD **Lat N52:00:51** **Long W00:40:22**

Road Directions

From the A5, on the southern outskirts of Milton Keynes: take the exit signposted for Denbigh North and Caldecotte, also signposted for the A4146. Take the 3rd exit on the roundabout from the south, or the 1st from the north, and continue eastwards along the H10 "Bletcham Way". At the first roundabout, named "Walton Park", head straight across. At the second roundabout head straight across again (this has V11, "Tongwell Street", heading north from it). At the end of H10 is another roundabout, take the 2nd exit, south, along Britten Grove. Take the 3rd right, along Boyce Crescent and follow this road round to Davenport Lea. Park somewhere near Davenport Lea, although not in the road itself and walk the length of Davenport Road. At the end of this road is a cycle way (or Red Route) turn right (south) along this clearly marked path and within minutes you will reach the gates across the line.

There is no official parking in the area but free on-street parking is available, although it is probably best to stick to the bigger roads, Boyce Crescent for example, rather than the little side roads.

2) 150102 rounds the corner from Woburn Sands, spending the day shuttling between Bedford and Bletchley.
August, 09:00, dslr@32mm

Northampton Loop

Passenger Traffic

The Northampton Loop section is solely in the hands of London Midland. These workings are operated mainly by 350 Desiro units but the occasional 321 will turn up. The Desiros are all based at Northampton's Kings Heath depot. The only real exception to this is Scot Rail's Caledonian Sleeper which runs in the early morning southbound or late evening northbound. Because of this it can only be viewed during the summer months.

1) 321430 heads south on the Northampton Loop.
Photo by Jason Rodhouse, July, 14:45, dslr@85mm

Freight Traffic

The West Coast Main Line is the preferred route from north to south so a wide variety of freight uses this line, with workings from all the freight operators. DB Schenker providrs motive power in the shape of 92, 66 and the occasional 90, Their traffic consists mainly of intermodal traffic with some Enterprise, Automotive and Cement traffic adding to the mix. Freightliner traffic is purely based around their intermodal traffic. Serving destinations as varied as Tilbury, Felixstowe, Ditton, Garston and Coatbridge. There are also a number of intermodal workings with DRS in charge, heading to the 'Daventry International Rail Freight Terminal' or DRIFT just to the south of Rugby. This traffic is either the 'Malcoms' or Tesco branded workings. They also operate their flask trains along this route but these run during the hours of darkness.
GBRf operates a number of intermodal trains between Hams Hall and Felixstowe. In addition to this, they operate, on behalf of the Royal Mail, their 325 units conveying mail between Willesden and Shieldmuir or Warrington. These workings can often be assisted by class 87 locomotives.
New operator Colas also operates a Hams Hall to Dollands Moor intermodal that continues on through the Channel Tunnel.

2) 90016 on a southbound intermodal, Barby Nortoft.
Photo by Jason Rodhouse, April, 07:45, dslr@36mm

Occasional Traffic

There are frequent charters along this route. The New Measurement train is diagrammed to visit the line on Tuesdays, Wednesdays and Thursdays. In addition there is the 'as required' other Serco traffic. With the Kings Heath Desiro depot there are infrequent hauled stock deliveries after units have been away for heavy maintenance.

3) 66138 hauls 350263 to Northampton,Milton Malsor.
July, 11:00, slr@50mm

Northampton Loop

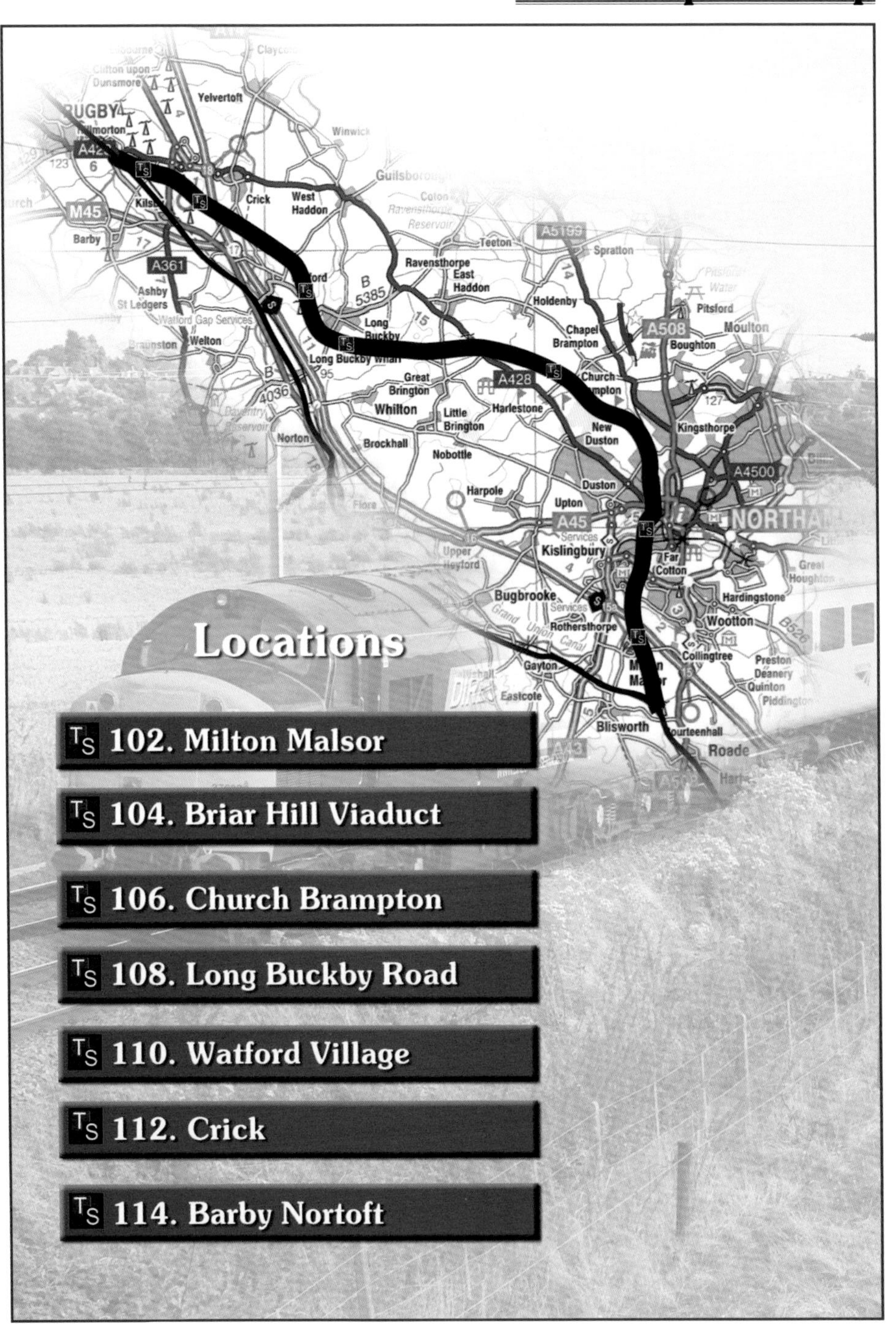

Milton Malsor

Location Notes

Milton Malsor is a quiet village on the outskirts of Northampton. This particular location is in a field with a footpath running under the railway to give easy access to both sides.

1) Taken with a step ladder from the field edge, 86501 heads north towards Northampton with a liner for Scotland.
Photo by Jason Rodhouse, April, 16:30. dslr@40mm

Public Transport

Stagecoach, services 88/X88 operate every 30 minutes from Northampton Bus Station with alternate journeys extending to Milton Keynes and a few to Oxford. All of these call at Milton Malsor. Alternatively, Stagecoach, service 89 operates hourly from Northampton to Milton Malsor and continues to Milton Keynes. The buses stop at 'The Memorial' on the High Street, from where you can walk west to Stockwell Road and then follow it round to Stockwell Way.

Amenities

Not a village with many facilities, although there is a post office/stores shop. There are plenty of pubs in the surrounding area and motorway services at Junction 15A of the M1.

Accommodation

The Hilton Hotel and the Queen Eleanor Hotel further up the A45 are only a few minutes away.

Photographic notes

The footpath through the field to the east of the line offers wider shots of southbound traffic during the morning. The field to the west affords some tighter angles in both directions. But if shooting from this side a step ladder will be advantageous as lineside vegetation often encroaches on shots.

2) Taken with step ladders, 66574 takes a loaded modal south.
Photo by Jason Roadhouse, February, 14:15, dslr@50mm

Milton Malsor

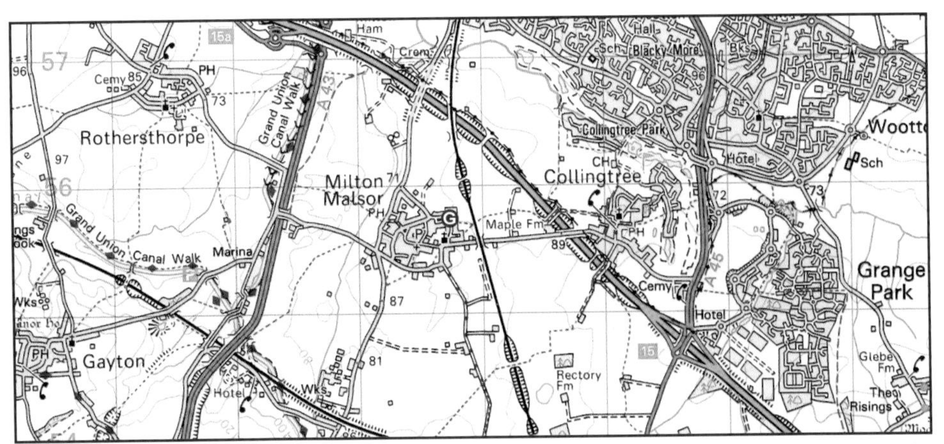

Postcode: NN7 3AL **Lat N52:11:41** **Long W00:55:12**

Road directions

From M1 junction 15: head towards Northampton on the A45. Turn left just after the Hotel into Watering Lane and follow this road. You will eventually pass over the motorway and will soon pass under the railway as you enter Milton Malsor. In the village turn right into Church Close then left into Stockwell Way and park here. From Stockwell Way there are three access points to the public footpath which leads to the location. Take the path which passes under the railway.

3) 90044 heads south with a liner for Felixstowe, taken from the field to the east of the line.
Photo by Jason Rodhouse, October, 09:15, dslr@36mm

Briar Hill, 15 Arches Viaduct, Northampton

Location Notes

Briar Hill is an estate to the south of Northampton Castle Station. This location is a canal towpath to one side and open grassland to the north of the canal. The canal stretch normally only sees anglers and the occasional resident walking their dog. Although normally quite quiet, care should be taken at all times.

1) A freightliner 66 heads south with a liner for Tilbury as seen from the southern edge of the canal.
Photo by Jason Rodhouse, November, 10:45, dslr@30mm

Public Transport

First Group,service 12 runs between Northampton Bus Station and Ashbrow Road in Briar Hill. From there head north to Thorn Hill Road. Turn right and follow this road up to Ring Way and then take the footpath to the canal. You will see the bridge to your right.

Amenities

There is nothing in the immediate area but the Briar Hill estate does have some local shops, including a fish and chip shop. Failing that, Northampton town centre should have everything you need.

Photographic Notes

Views are very limited these days due to excessive growth of the lineside shrubbery, so best avoided at times of plant growth. However, a few shots can still be had here, a step ladder would be an advantage. The best shots are of southbound trains which can be photographed from the eastern side of the line in the mornings and these can be had until early lunchtime. This shot can be taken from the canal side, and a similar shot from between the canal and the river. There are also a couple of footbridges crossing the river that offer views from the west side of the line.

2) 86612 leads 614 with a 66 in tow across the bridge.
Photo by Jason Rodhouse, September, 18:00, dslr@60mm

Briar Hill, 15 Arches Viaduct, Northampton

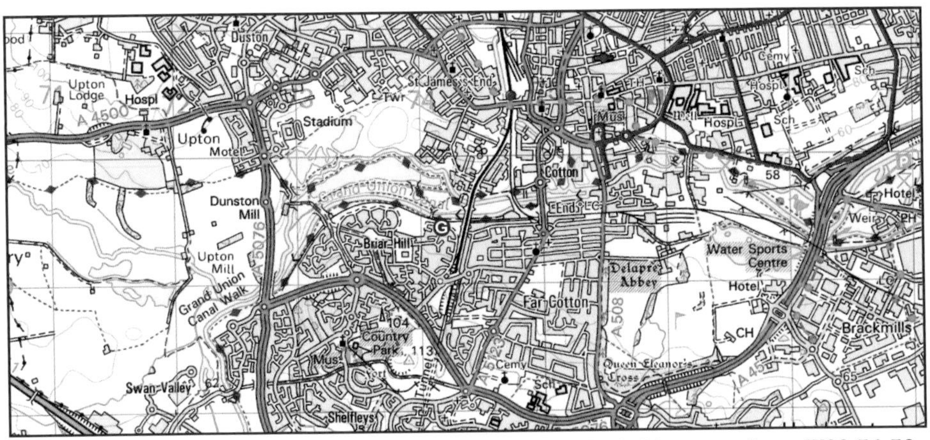

Postcode: NN4 8SJ **Lat N52:13:46** **Long W00:54:50**

Road Directions

From M1 Junction 15: head north towards Northampton on the A45. Continue until you reach the junction where you meet the A45 West (Mere Way).
Take Mere Way and keep heading west, turning right (4th exit) at the next large roundabout. You will soon pass a playing field on your right. Here you need to look for a left turn, Rothersthorpe Road. Follow this road, going straight over a small roundabout, and you will soon come to another roundabout, at which you need the third exit - Ringway. Follow this road to the end and park. On the opposite side from the houses there is a footpath which crosses the old railway line which has recently been lifted (2005?) The canal is a short distance further on. Follow the canal to the right for one of the shots which can be had here, or follow the path over the bridge to your right, and this will take you to the other shots.

There is plenty of room to park at the bottom of Ringway, but do remember to lock up and use crook locks etc if you have them.

3) With a local London Midland working, 350126 heads south towards Milton Keynes.
Photo by Jason Rodhouse, September, 11:45, dslr@24mm

Church Brampton

Location Notes

The location is in a field, through which a bridleway passes, between the villages of Church Brampton and Harlestone in rural Northamptonshire.

1) 57006 hauls a lightly loaded liner south.
Photo by Jason Rodhouse, February, 13:30, dslr@39mm

Public Transport

Stagecoach's service 96 runs from Northampton Railway Station to Church Brampton Village every other hour during the day. It would then be a 20 minute walk to the location.

Amenities

'The Fox and Hounds', formerly 'The Dusty Fox' in Harlestone provides good food and drink.

Photographic Notes

Shots can be taken in both directions. 'Closer-up' shots can also be taken from the lineside fence, giving you a range of shooting options.
The tree in view 3, by the second wagon, is now bigger and there is also a small track side box around the third or fourth wagon position.

2) 66540 seen across the fields heads towards London.
Photo by Jason Rodhouse, March, 14:00, dslr@30mm

Church Brampton

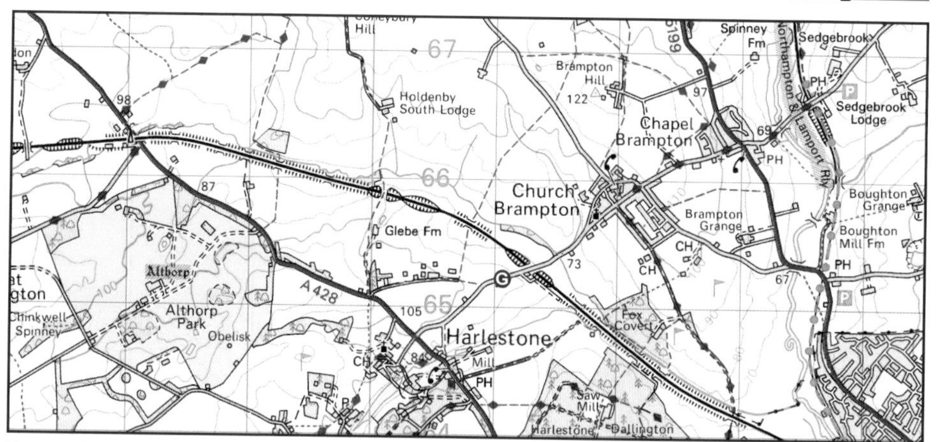

Postcode: NN6 8AR **Lat N52:17:04** **Long W00:57:49**

Road Directions

From M1 Junction 16: take the exit and head east on the A45 towards Northampton. After about 2½ miles take the first exit at the roundabout (Sandy Lane). After about 2 miles turn left onto Port Lane and then right onto White Lane and left on the A428. After about a mile you will pass through Harlestone. Note the pub on the right, 'The Fox and Hounds' and perhaps more importantly, the speed camera on the left. As you leave Harlestone and the road begins to climb, look out for a right hand turning signposted 'The Bramptons'. Take this turn and follow the road until it kinks to the right. You will see room to park 2-3 cars on the left. If you cross the railway, you have gone too far.

There are actually two similar places on the short stretch of road and this could cause confusion. Parking is literally off the road as it kinks to the right and the railway will be seen from this point. Look for an area to park 2-3 cars.

3) 60026 takes the Bletchley to Peak Forest stone empties back up the West Coast Main Line.
Photo by Jason Rodhouse, February, 11:45, dslr@42mm

Long Buckby Road

Location Notes

Situated between Watford and Long Buckby this location, also know locally as Murcott, is in a quiet field.

1) Catching the early morning light 350104 heads south on a London Midland Birmingham to Euston service.
Photo by Jason Rodhouse, March, 08:00, dslr@24mm

Public Transport

Long Buckby station is served by two trains an hour from Birmingham to Northampton, hourly continuing through to London Euston. Stagecoach service 96 operates hourly between Rugby and Northampton and runs along the B5385 between Watford and Long Buckby.

Amenities

There are plenty of pubs and shops in Long Buckby village.

Photographic Notes

Photos can be taken from both sides of the line as there is a public footpath which passes under the tracks.
However, the light conditions play an important part. The best shot to be had is facing north in the afternoon. For this, you need to walk diagonally over the small field to the fence. However, no northbound shots can be taken from this point as a large tree blocks the view.

2) 86604 and 637 double up on a southbound intermodal.
Photo by Jason Rodhouse, September, 17:00, dslr@40mm

Long Buckby Road

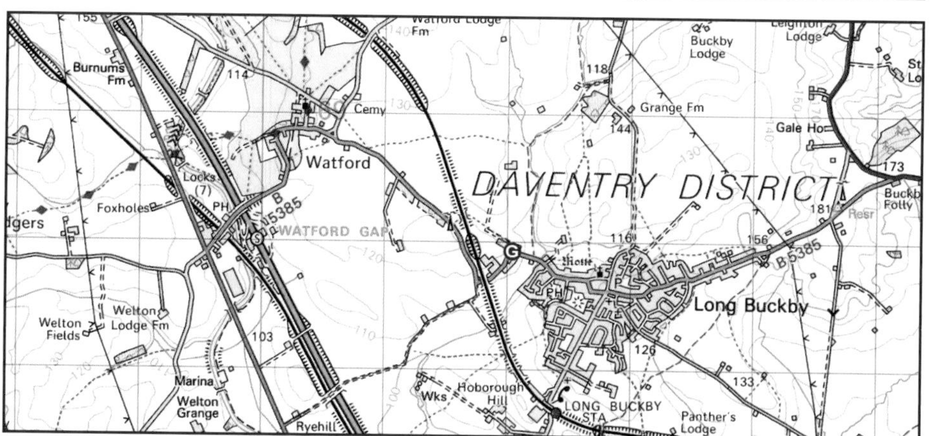

Postcode: NN6 7QR **Lat N52:18:32** **Long W01:05:51**

Road Directions

From M1 Junction 16: take the exit and head east on the A45 towards Northampton. After about 2½ miles take the first exit at the roundabout (Sandy Lane). After about 2 miles turn left onto Port Lane and then right onto White Lane and left on the A428. The turning for Long Buckby is well signposted. In the centre of the village, turn into King Street and continue on the B5385. After passing under the railway the road bends to the right. Shortly after this there is a double gate and a public footpath sign on the right hand side.

If you are careful you can park a car here without blocking the gates.

3) 56302 takes a lightly loaded Fastline intermodal south to the Isle of Grain.
Photo by Jason Rodhouse, August, 16:45, dslr@24mm

Watford Village

Location Notes

Watford Village is a small Northamptonshire village and is a short distance from Long Buckby.
A public footpath leads to the location and then over the line by means of a foot crossing. Please be wary of the cattle and unprotected barbed wire.

1) 37602 with a Serco overhead line test train heads north towards Rugby.
Photo by Jason Rodhouse, July, 16:45, dslr@39mm

Public Transport

Stagecoach service 96 operates hourly between Rugby and Northampton to Watford Village and runs along the B5385 between Watford and Long Buckby.

Amenities

There is a restaurant in the village but you will be better catered for in nearby Long Buckby which has many shops and pubs.

Photographic Notes

Photos can be taken in both directions and from both sides of the line to suit lighting conditions.
The location is on the embankment that would have led up to a rail bridge that crossed the line but the bridge was removed many years ago. You can either shoot from the top of the embankment or from lower down but if you are not on the top you will not be able to see what is approaching from behind you. .

Watford Village

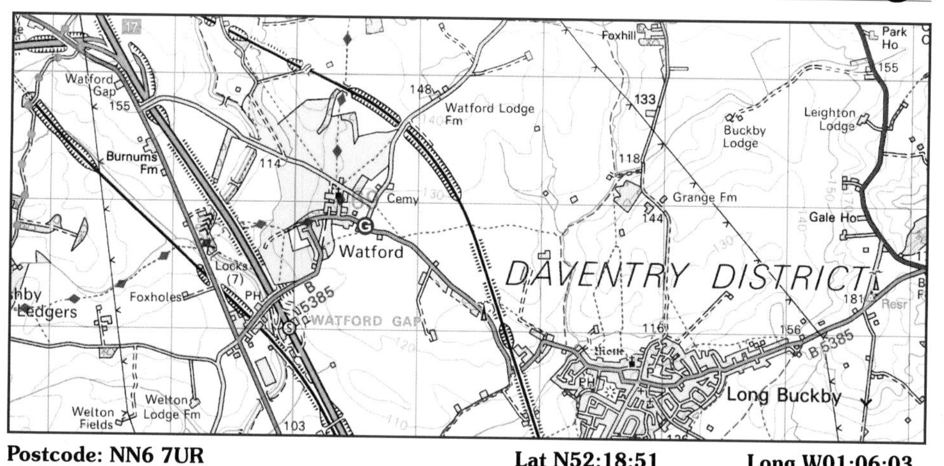

Postcode: NN6 7UR **Lat N52:18:51** **Long W01:06:03**

Road Directions

From M1 Junction 16: take the exit and head east on the A45 towards Northampton. After about 2½ miles take the first exit at the roundabout (Sandy Lane). After about 2 miles turn left onto Port Lane and then right onto White Lane and left on the A428. The turning for Long Buckby is well signposted. In Long Buckby, turn into King Street and continue on the B5385 heading for Watford Village. Just before you get to the village, you will notice a public footpath sign on the right and slightly further ahead you will notice a space on the left hand side where a few cars can be safely parked. Park here, making sure that you do not block the gates. Walk back to the public footpath and follow it around the field edge to the location. The location is in the clump of trees up the bank.

2) With a West Coast Railways southbound ECS move to Southall 37516 and 37676 catch the early afternoon sun.
June, 14:30 dslr@24mm

Crick

Location Notes

The location is a quiet field side location, where you may have the odd sheep or two for company, on the outskirts of Crick. Crick is just a short distance away from the 'DIRFT'. Locals muse that the DIRFT (Daventry International Rail Freight Terminal) should be the CIRFT (Crick International Rail Freight Terminal) as it is not anywhere near Daventry, which is 6 miles away.

1) 92016 'Brahms' passes Crick with a southbound Bescot to Wembley enterprise working.
Photo by Jason Rodhouse, May, 15:30 dslr@32mm

Public Transport

Stagecoach service 96 runs between Rugby North Street and Northampton Railway Station Bridge. It calls in Crick opposite 'The Wheatsheaf' pub on the Main Road. From there walk west back down Main Road and you will see the lane to the location turning off next left after 'The Derry'.

Amenities

Around the DIRFT site there are a few petrol stations, and 'burger van' type outlets can often be found.

Accommodation

There is an Ibis hotel just off the M1, Junction 18.

Photographic notes

This location is best for southbound shots from late morning through to the afternoon, with northbound shots from late afternoon through the evening. Shots can also be had from a distance within the field and also from the line side fence. Due to the very close proximity of the M1 motorway this spot is far from ideal for those who wish to take video.

2) 86604 and 628 head south on an intermodal to Felixstowe.
Photo by Jason Rodhouse, May, 16:30 dslr@39mm

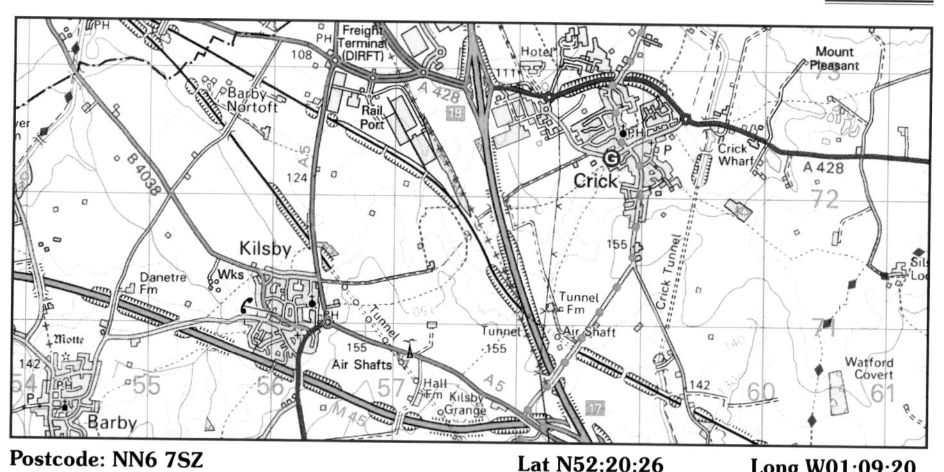

Postcode: NN6 7SZ **Lat N52:20:26** **Long W01:09:20**

Road Directions

From M1 Junction 18: take the A428 east and continue past the industrial units until you enter the village. After passing Bucknills Lane on the left look for a lane on the right which will lead you to the location. At the end of the lane take the footpath which passes under the motorway and then under the railway lines and brings you out into the field.

The lane leading down to the location is far from suitable for most road vehicles so it may be best to park on the main road and walk the full distance. There is a very high risk of damage to your vehicle or even grounding as the road surface is VERY uneven. The lane is is often waterlogged so wellies may be a good idea if there has been recent wet weather.

3) 86501 heads north with a Felixstowe to Trafford Park intermodal working.
Photo by Jason Rodhouse, May, 15:30 dslr@24mm

Barby Nortoft

Location Notes

Barby Nortoft is in Northamptonshire, just a short distance away from the 'DIRFT'. The location itself is an overbridge on a quiet country road.

1) 56311 heads north with a Dollands Moor-Hams Hall intermodal working.
Photo by Jason Rodhouse, July, 17:30, dslr@50mm

Public Transport

Stagecoach service 96 runs between Rugby North Street and Northampton Railway Station Bridge. It stops opposite Lennon Close, west of the location and at 'Celtic Way' in the DIRFT. From either of these locations it would then be a 15-20 minute walk to the location.

Amenities

There is nothing at the location but If you continue along the A428 you will reach Northampton which has plenty of shops and take-aways. You will pass a 'Hungry Horse' pub just after passing under the railway lines. Kilsby village, to the south, has 'The Red Lion' and 'The George' public houses which serve excellent real ales and the 'Hunt House Quarters' restaurant.

Accommodation

There is an Ibis hotel just off the M1, Junction 18. 'The George' in Kilsby also offers accommodation.

Photographic Notes

Photos can be taken from both sides of the bridge. If you leave the bridge and go down hill slightly you will see a gate. This is the entrance to Lodge Farm. You will be able to get a wide shot from here. On the opposite side of the road there is a small gap in the hedge. Southbound shots can be taken from here.

Barby Nortoft

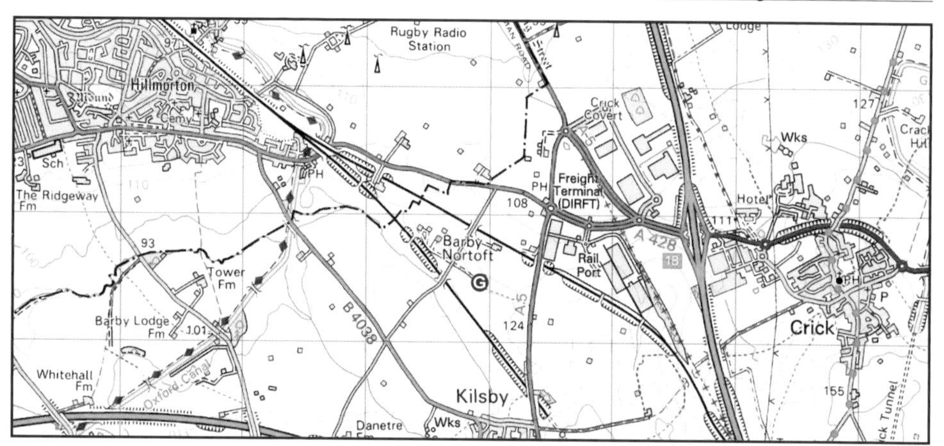

Postcode: CV23 8YF **Lat N52:21:05** **Long W01:10:52**

Road Directions

From M1 Junction 18: follow the signs towards Rugby on the A428. You will shortly come to a roundabout, which you should go straight over. There is a pub on the right, and a UK petrol station on the left. Shortly after this, take the next left. Not far down this quiet road is the location.

You can park to the left of the bridge.

3) 66417 reaches the end of it's journey at Daventry with a working from Grangemouth.
Photo by Scott Borthwick, March, 13:45, slr@48mm

Bletchley to Birmingham (Main Line)

Passenger Traffic

Two regular operators use this route: Virgin Trains and London Midland.
London Midland use predominantly Desiro Class 350 units, with the occasional 321 on it's local services.
Virgin Trains are operated by Pendolino Class 390 EMUs and Voyager class 221 DEMUs although they

1) A fortunate combination of boat, rainbow and a Virgin Pendolino. Passing Shilton, heading towards Rugby.
August, 18:15, dslr@24mm

also have a standby MkIII set, re-livered into the same colour scheme as the Pendolinos, that operates as a stand-in when there are not enough 390s available. This is then timetabled to do a number of peak hour services. The DVT is usually at the London end with a DB Schenker class 90 providing power at the country end.

2) 60084 heads north pasing Cathiron.
September, 16:00, dslr@85mm

Freight Traffic

Little freight traffic uses the section of the route south of Rugby as it is all pathed via the Northampton Loop. This is due to the lack of low speed paths along this section of the line. At Rugby there are now four tracks along a good section. Intermodal; cement and enterprise workings can be expected from all the major operators as per the traffic for the Northampton Loop.

Occasional Traffic

There are frequent charters along this route. The New Measurement train is diagrammed to visit the line on Tuesdays, Wednesdays and Thursdays. In addition there is the 'as required' other Serco traffic.
With it's base at Wolverton, to the north of Bletchley, the Royal Train is also an unpredictable, but regular, visitor to this section of line.

3) 66723 south through Rugby with a stock move.
Photo by Jason Rodhouse, June 10:30, dslr@30mm

Bletchley to Birmingham

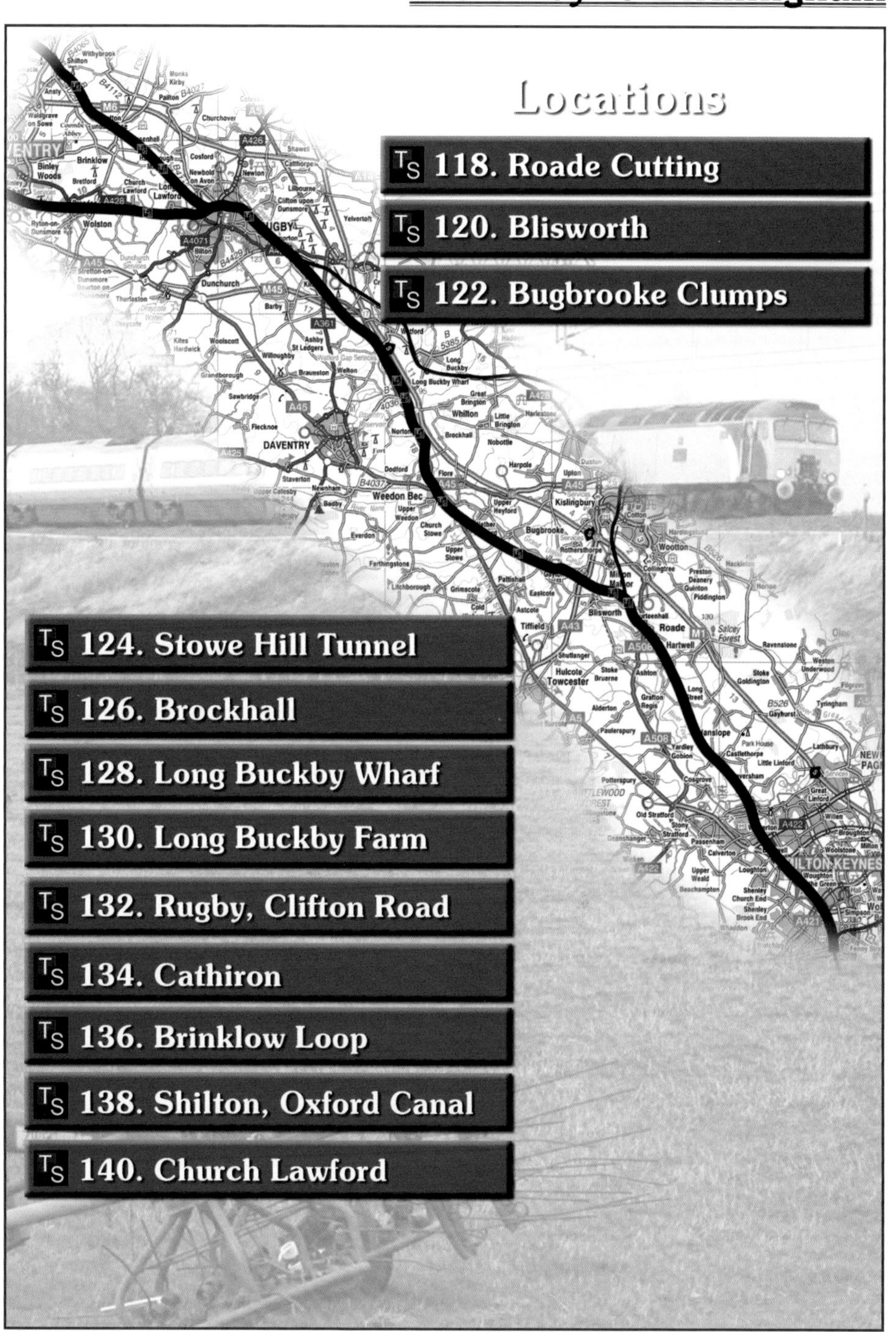

Roade Cutting

Location Notes

These quiet bridges are on the outskirts of Roade in the open countryside. Neither bridge carries normal road traffic as both are green lane type ways but you might get a farm vehicle occasionally.
The location is on the busy West Coast Main Line just to the south of Northampton.
The four tracks split here with two lines diverting via the Northampton Loop while the 'main' lines avoid Northampton, heading north via Weedon.

1) 92031 works south with the 6L42 Warrington Arpley-Ripple Lane.
Photo by Jason Rodhouse, July, 15:15, dslr@18mm

Public Transport

Stagecoach Cross Country service X4 operates hourly from Milton Keynes Railway Station to Hyde Road in Roade. From Hyde Road walk east to the main road (A508 - London Road) and turn left and walk up to Bailey Brooks Lane, marked by a 'bottle bank/village hall' sign. Turn up here and then follow the road directions.

Amenities

There are a couple of small stores, a chinese takeaway/fish and chip shop and a pub in the village.

Photographic Notes

This is a classic location and whilst perhaps not the prettiest of landscapes it is an interesting view. The location is difficult for photography and may present a challenge for some. The tracks are deep in the cutting here, so you can expect very long shadows. There is also no easy way of avoiding the overhead catenary, but it does at least offer a different perspective. Given the deep nature of the cutting, light will be better towards the middle of the day when the sun is high in the sky. The sun should be in the best position between the hours of 10.00 and 16.00.

Roade Cutting

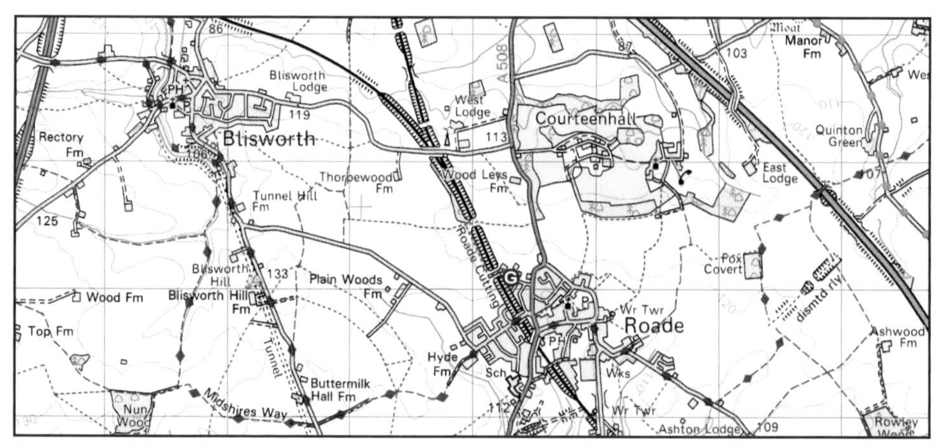

Postcode: NN7 2PT **Lat N52:09:57** **Long W00:54:18**

Road Directions

From M1 Junction 15: head south on the A508 towards Stoke Bruerne. After a couple of miles, you will reach Roade. Take the first turning on the right into Bailey Brooks Lane. This turning is also marked by a 'bottle bank/village hall' sign. Follow this road to the end and park, considerately, by the private road/ footpath. Walk up the 'private road' and on the left, after the last house, is a gate which leads to the southern bridge. Although you can go straight on over style/gap in fence which leads up the field to the middle bridge, this is not a footpath just a field edge, so it is better to use the southern bridge to cross the line and walk up the footpath to the northern bridge.

2) 66715 heads north on a Felixstowe to Hams Hall modal.
Photo by Jason Rodhouse, July, 14:45, dslr@24mm

Blisworth

Location Notes

The Is a rural location with good views of the line from a footbridge that spans the tracks and from the adjoining fields. It is also sometimes referred to as Milton Crossing.

1) 390048 heading south, seen from the footpath across the fields to the north of the bridge location.
Photo by Mark Bearton, May, 15:30, dslr@50mm

Public Transport

Stagecoach services 88/X88 operate every 30 minutes from Northampton Bus Station with alternate journeys extending to Milton Keynes and a few to Oxford, these call in Blisworth village. Alternatively Stagecoach service 89, also operates hourly from Northampton to Blisworth and continues on to Milton Keynes. It will be about a ¾ mile walk from the village to the location.

Amenities

The location is rural, set in fields and there are no amenities. The nearest habitation is the village of Blisworth itself, with a village store and a couple of pubs. Northampton is a large town where you should find anything you might need. It is approximately five miles by road.

2) 390009 heads north, seen from the north side of the bridge.
June, 11:30, dslr@24mm

Photographic Notes

The preferred shot at this location is of northbound workings. For these, the light will be better from early afternoon onwards. The southbound shot, from the southern side of the bridge, has been spoiled by a new signal placed a few metres away from the bridge. This only leaves a southbound shot from the north side of the bridge, which would only be well lit in the summer months before 09.00. The footpath to the north also offers shots in both directions.

The area is away from any sources of noise that would cause problems for videography.

Blisworth

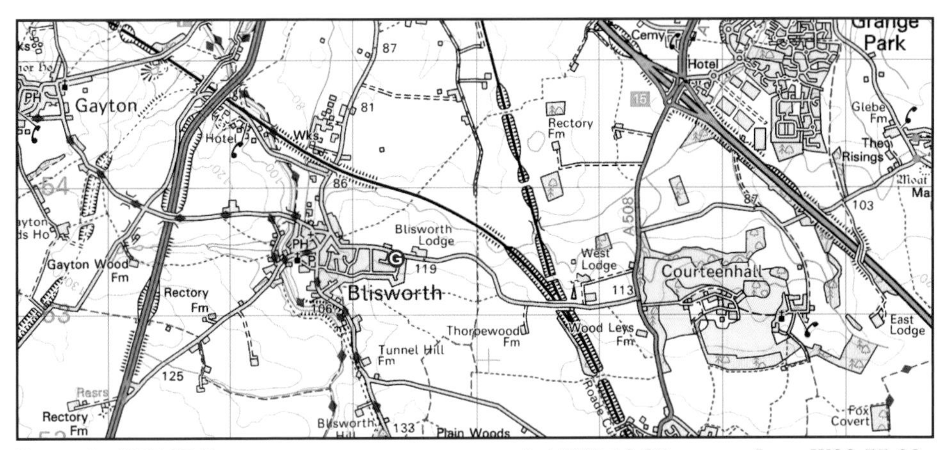

Postcode: NN7 3DG **Lat N52:10:35** **Long W00:55:09**

Road Directions

From M1 Junction 15: take the A508 south towards Stony Stratford. After approximately 1 mile take a right turn up an unclassified road heading for Blisworth. After a short while you will cross over the main line and after approximately 200 yards there is a track on the right heading downhill towards a metal footbridge. This follows a row of trees along a field border. There is an area of verge at the entrance to the track where it is possible to park a car and there is room to park a few cars on the opposite side of the road.

Occasionally contractors use this track to gain access to the lines so please do not block the access to the track itself. There is room to park a few cars off-road on the opposite side of the road.

3) 90028 heads north towards Birmingham with the spare Virgin MkIII set standing in for a Pendolino.
Photo by Mark Bearton, May, 16:30, dslr@40mm

Bugbrooke Clumps

Location Notes

Bugbrooke is a peaceful village in rural Northamptonshire. This particular location, also known by some as Bugbrooke Downs, is a field.

1) 573xx heads south past the level crossing. This view, from Banbury Lane, was taken using a step ladder to get over a hedge. *Photo by Jason Roadhouse, February, 10:15, dslr@60mm*

Public Transport

Stagecoach service D3 operates hourly from the bridge outside Northampton Railway Station to Bugbrooke Village. It enters the village from the north and turns right in the village where you will need to get off to walk to the location.

Amenities

Bugbrooke has a small local convenience store and two pubs.

Photographic Notes

The best shots are looking east from the field. If you want a shot looking west you will need to walk round the field edge.
A quiet location, so video would not be a problem, apart from perhaps bleating lambs and at other times of the year, moo-ing cows!

2) Sheep prefer classic traction, ignoring a northbound 390. *Photo by Jason Rodhouse, March, 13:00, dslr@35mm*

Bugbrooke Clumps

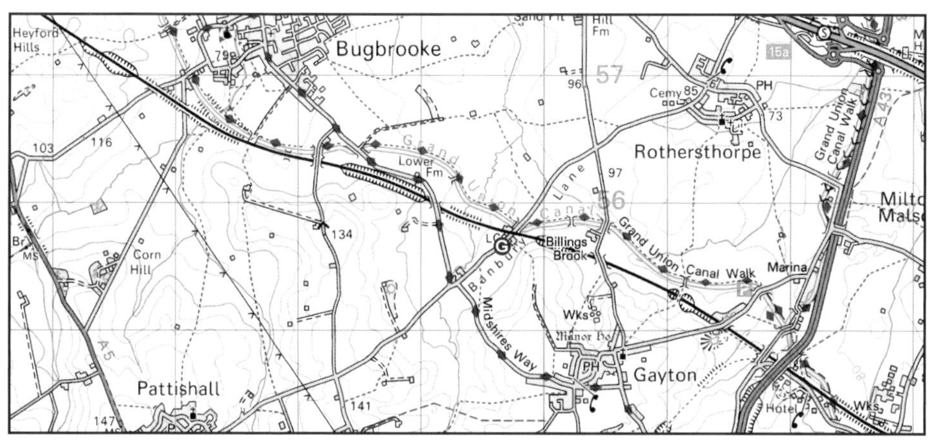

Postcode: NN7 3JF **Lat N52:11:47** **Long W00:59:21**

Road Directions

From M1, junction 15A: follow the signs to Rothersthorpe. Pass through the village, and you will shortly come to the new overbridge which crosses the railway line. Continue on this road, passing the left turn to Gayton and take the right turn to Bugbrooke. The entrance to the field is a few hundred yards on your right. If you cross over the railway you have gone too far.

Park by the field entrance but do not block the gates.

3) 90036 with an afternoon Birmingham working.
Photo by Jason Rodhouse, April, 16:30, dslr@36mm

Stowe Hill Tunnel, Weedon

Location Notes

Weedon is a village in Northamptonshire, the location itself is in quiet country fields near the canal.

1) 90020 with a northbound working to Birmingham.
Photo by Jason Rodhouse, August, xx:xx, dslr@xxmm

Public Transport

Daventry Dart services D1 and D2 run from Northampton Railway Station to Weedon, calling opposite the Wheatsheaf pub (A5/A45 crossroads). Cross the High Street and follow the Canal Towpath south. When you reach the next canal bridge you are at the location.

Amenities

There is nothing at the location but Weedon village has a few pubs, a One-stop store and a sandwich shop. There are also two restaurants at the cross-roads, and there is a chinese takeaway here. Otherwise Daventry is about five miles away with a full range of facilities.

2) 82146 south, this shot is through the bridge fence.
Photo by Jason Rodhouse, April, 15:15, dslr@52mm

Accommodation

There are two hotels at the crossroads 'The Globe' and 'The Crossroads'.

Photographic Notes

The best shot here is of the northbound trains. Sunny afternoons are best for the ideal shot. Shots can also be taken from the overbridge but don`t expect fantastic results, or from the canal but the line here is too far away for even reasonable results. Depending on wind direction, location should be quiet enough for people wishing to take video footage. The A5 can sometimes be noisy but nothing too serious.

Stowe Hill Tunnel, Weedon

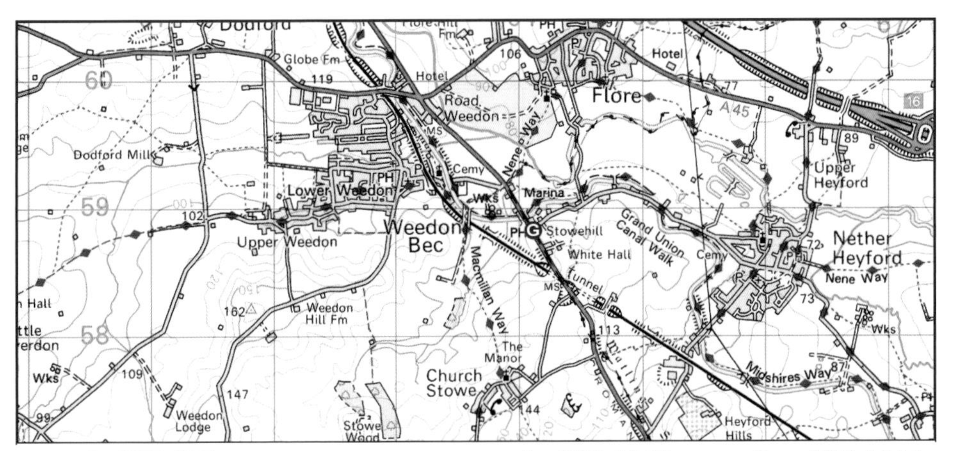

Postcode: NN7 4RZ **Lat N52:13:23** **Long W01:04:16**

Road Directions

Weedon village is on the A45/A5 crossroads. To get to the location from the crossroads, head towards Towcester/Milton Keynes on the A5. As you go up the hill you will notice 'Clarke Bros' garage on your left. Opposite this is a right hand turn. Take this turning and park on the hard standing which is almost immediately on the left.

From here walk up the track which is clearly visible The track also leads to the sewerage works. Keep following the track and you will soon see the canal bridge. Cross the bridge and follow the public footpath. You will eventually find a large gap in the bushes on the left hand side. You will be able to see the shot from here.

It is best to park as described above. If you have a vehicle which is higher off the ground you can drive a little further and park by the canal bridge. However, it is best to play safe and stretch those legs.

3) 87002 emerges from the tunnel and heads north with a Euston to Birmingham New Street Virgin working.
Photo by Scott Borthwick, July, 17:45, dslr@60mm

Brockhall

Location Notes

Brockhall is a very quiet field location in rural Northamptonshire.

1) 350124 heads south with a London Midland local service to London Euston.
Photo by Jason Rodhouse, March, 13:45, dslr@52mm

Public Transport

Stagecoach, services D1/D2 (direct) or D3 (via Bugbrooke) operate three times an hour from Northampton Station to Weedon crossroads from where it would be about a 25 to 30 minute walk along the A5 to the location.

Amenities

There are no amenities at the location. However, there is a 'One-stop' shop in Weedon village centre near the church as well as a sandwich shop and a few pubs. There is also a chinese takeaway in the village. Further along the A5, in the Towcester direction, there is a petrol station with a coffee shop. The Heart of the Shires shopping village has some places to eat.

2) 37609 and 37606 top and tail an OLE test train south to London.
Photo by Jason Rodhouse, September, 18:00, dslr@33mm

Photographic Notes

Although shots can be taken in both directions, this location is ideal for afternoon northbound shots. You may prefer to walk down the field edge for variations on the location.

Brockhall

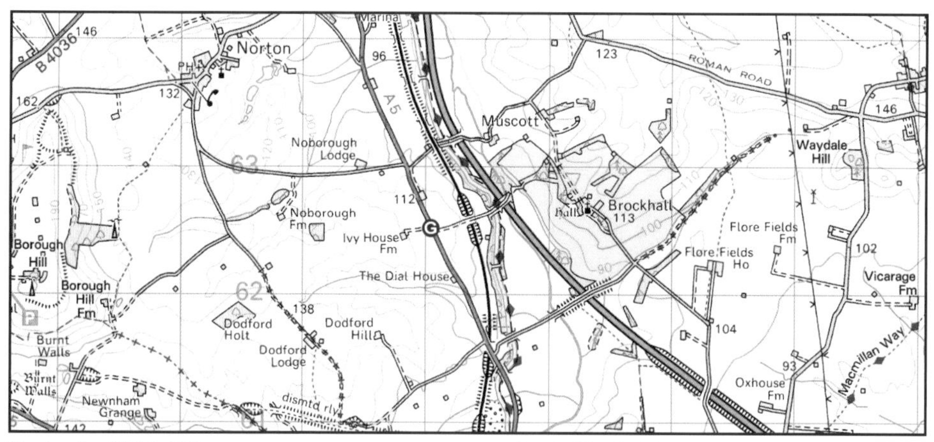

Postcode: NN7 4LB **Lat N52:15:21** **Long W01:05:15**

Road Directions

Brockhall is off the A5 between Weedon and Kilsby. From Weedon, ignoring any signs for Brockhall Village, head down the A5 towards Lutterworth. After passing two turns to Dodford on the left, look out for 'The Dial House' on the left. Take the right hand turn shortly after this. There is a 'weight limit' sign by the gate. Heading down the narrow track you will come to the bridge which crosses the railway.

Park your car on the right hand side of the track before the bridge.

3) 90021 with the MkIII set heads north to Birmingham.
Photo by Jason Rodhouse, May, 17:45, dslr@28mm

Whilton and Long Buckby Wharf

Location Notes

Long Buckby Wharf is just south west of Long Buckby village. The M1, canal, and WCML are within close proximity to each other here, with the railway actually crossing the canal at this particular location which can be very busy with tourists at times.

1) An unidentified 390 heads south towards London, passing the queue of river traffic on the Grand Union canal.
Photo by Jason Rodhouse, April, 09:30, dslr@24mm

Public Transport

The wharf is a relatively short walk from Long Buckby station, down Station Road. The station is served by two trains an hour from Birmingham to Northampton, hourly continuing to London Euston.
Stagecoach, service 96, also operates hourly between
Buckby village.

Amenities

Whilton Locks has a garden centre and restaurant. There is also a private cafe alongside the canal which offers cream teas at certain times of the year.
Long Buckby village also has lots to offer. The 'New Inn' on the A5 is recommended for its great selection of beer and outstanding meals.

Photographic Notes

This location can provide something a little different, to break the monotony of similar looking Pendolino shots. Although mostly suited to morning shots, an alternative summer shot of the bridge crossing the canal can be had from about 16.30 onwards.
If you follow the canal towpath south you will find plenty of opportunities for canal and railway shots.
The proximity to the M1 motorway will affect audio on video recordings..

2) A 390 heads north over the Grand Union.
Jason Rodhouse, June, 11:40, dslr@22mm

Whilton and Long Buckby Wharf

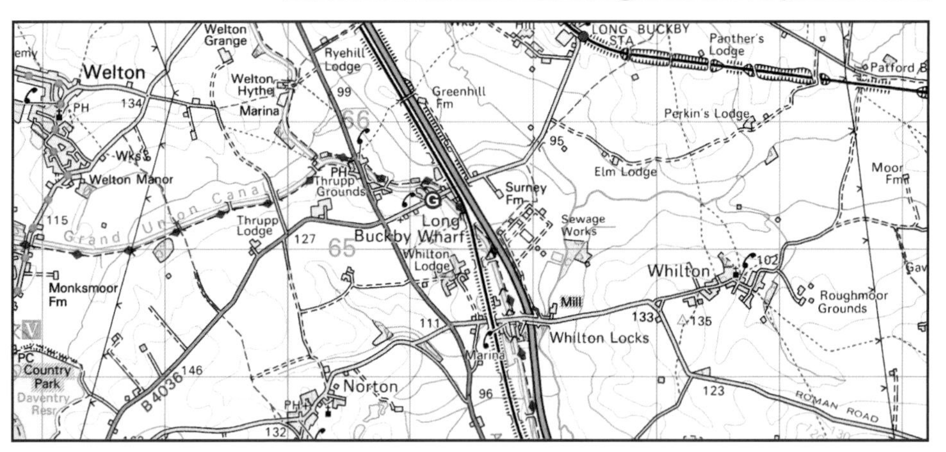

Postcode: NN6 7PP **Lat N52:16:57** **Long W01:06:05**

Road Directions

From M1 Junction 18: head to Kilsby. At the roundabout at Kilsby take the A5 turning to Milton Keynes. Continue down the A5 until you see 'The New Inn' on your right as you cross the canal. Turn left at the junction just ahead. As you near the railway and motorway bridges ahead, you will notice an area on the right hand side where you can park your car. The canal passes under the road just a few yards further ahead. Walk down to the canal to reach the location.

If you can, please park as described above. Do not park in the road opposite to this, as although it looks like a dwelling, the building is actually a doctor's surgery and space is often needed to assist elderly patients in and out of vehicles.

3) 90008 heading south with a Birmingham to London express, crosses the Grand Union canal at the Wharf.
Photo by Jason Rodhouse, June, 17:15, dslr@40mm

Long Buckby, Greenhill Farm

Location Notes

If it was not for the nearby M1, this would be a quiet rural location on the outskirts of Long Buckby. The location itself is at the end of a couple of fields, the first field is normally home to cattle..... so be wary when there are young calves about.

1) With the M1 in the background 90028 heads north with some former mail coaches.
Photo by Jason Rodhouse, December, 11:45, dslr@70mm

Public Transport

Long Buckby station is served by two trains an hour from Birmingham to Northampton, hourly continuing to London Euston. Stagecoach service 96 also operates hourly between Rugby and Northampton to Long Buckby village. From the village walk down Station Road and just before you cross the motorway there is a road which leads down to the location.

Amenities

'The New Inn' on the opposite side of the road is highly recommended. They serve meals, generously filled baguettes, and perhaps more importantly, have real ales on tap!

2) A Pendolino speeds north on it's journey to Manchester.
Photo by Jason Rodhouse, June, 15:15, dslr@48mm

Photographic Notes

This location is only good for southbound trains from about 12.00 as there is no shot from the east side of the line. Northbound trains can be shot from about 15.00, again from the west side of the bridge only. The Motorway verge is heavily tree lined and does not offer any shot of a train with the road traffic.
Shots can be taken from the approach to the bridge and also from across the fields.
Given the obvious proximity to the M1, video sound tracks will be heavily affected by traffic noise.

Long Buckby, Greenhill Farm

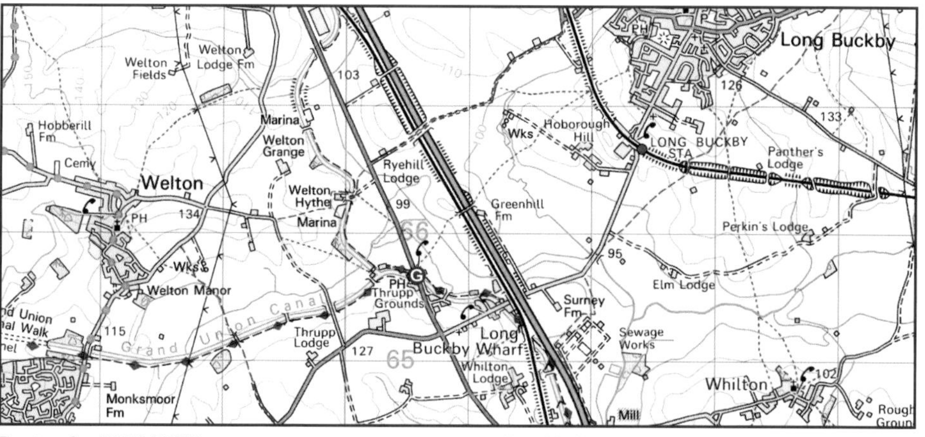

Postcode: NN6 7PW **Lat N52:17:24** **Long W01:06:30**

Road Directions

From M1 Junction 18: head to Kilsby. At the roundabout at Kilsby take the A5 turning to Milton Keynes. Continue down the A5. Shortly after crossing the canal pull into the parking area on the left hand side. If you pass 'The New Inn' on the right, you have gone too far. The pub is pretty much opposite the parking area. Just behind you on the same side of the road is a farm entrance. Although it says 'Ryehill Farm' this is the neighbouring farm, so do not worry, this is the right place. Go down here and pick up the public footpath which is clearly signposted. This will take you to the fields.

3) The newly repainted WB64 is pushed south by 90035, seen here passing the M1, heading for Euston.
Photo by Jason Rodhouse, 13:00, dslr@50mm

Rugby, Clifton Road

Location Notes

This location is just to the east of Rugby Station on a busy road bridge.
The shot is of a line used primarily by freight coming off the Northampton loop and flying over the West Coast Main Line to gain access to the slow lines but you can view all the lines.

1) 92017 slows on the approach to Rugby with a Wembley to Trafford Park Intermodal.
Photo by Jason Rodhouse, August, 15:00, dslr@40mm

Public Transport

Stagecoach service 2 operates regularly from Rugby North Street, but it is just as quick to walk to the location.

3) 350115 heads south towards Northampton.
Photo by Jason Rodhouse, August, 12:30, dslr@35mm

Amenities

There are a few local shops in the area and the 'Clifton Inn' is just down the road. The town centre is about a mile or so down the Clifton Road and should have anything else you might need.

Photographic Notes

Shots to the east are best in the afternoon. This shot was always quite limited and since the remodelling a new Overhead Line box mast has been erected making this, combined with the trees growing, even tighter. Shots to the west are generally best in the morning.
There is a tall barrier which divides the footpath and road here, so shooting on the west side of the bridge is fairly safe. However, for shots to the east, you need to be up against the bridge parapet and there is only about a foot between this and the road, so be careful. The location would not be good for video due to the noise of the passing traffic.

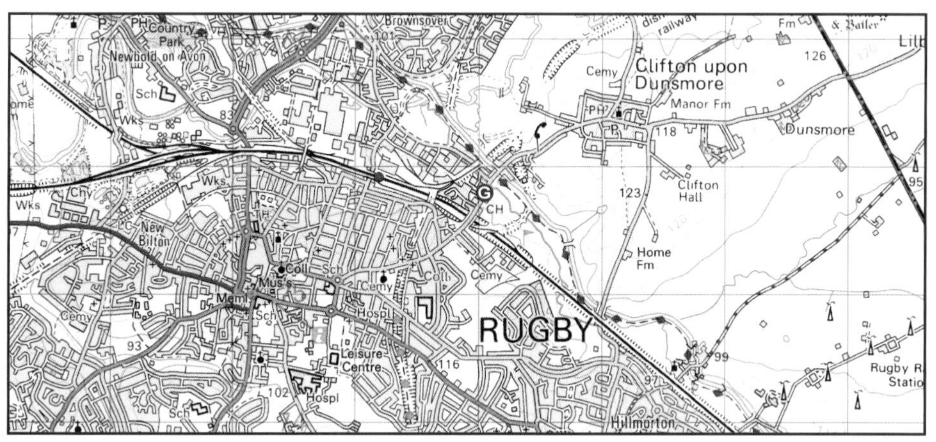

Postcode: CV21 3RD **Lat N52:22:33** **Long W01:14:18**

Road Directions

From Rugby station, head south (up the hill) along Murray Road. At the roundabout take the first exit down Clifton Road, the B5414 to Market Harborough. Keep following this road until you pass a playing field on your right. There are two turnings on the right after the playing field, before you reach the bridge. It is preferable to park in the second of these - Townsend Road.

3) 66573 crests the flyover with a Southampton to Crewe Basford Hall intermodal.
Photo by Jason Rodhouse, August, 15:45, dslr@50mm

Cathiron

Location Notes

The location is a bridge on a footpath joining Harborough Magna and Church Lawford, with a farm to the south. It is a popular location and there will often be other enthusiasts about, especially during the afternoons and evenings. All the lines are bi-directional here. During the West Coast Main Line's upgrades this section was upgraded from three to four tracks.

1) 90041 on the slow line, with a northbound intermodal from Felixstowe to Crewe, taken with a step ladder.
June, 16:45, dslr@55mm

Public Transport

De Courcey Travel service 585 runs between Rugby North Street and Harborough Magna, from where it would be a 20-30 minute walk to the location either along roads or via the footpaths.

Amenities

None close to hand, although there is an award winning chip shop in Brownsover, Rugby. This is about three miles away.

Photographic Notes

As the line runs south east to north west the sun is not usually on the right side for the footbridge shots until the afternoon. It is then good for 'sun on the nose' southbound shots until around 15.00 in summer. From then the northbound shot comes into its own until late evening. However, shadows from the trees affect the line.
Since the fourth track is about five feet from the edge of the bridge railings, a new palisade fence has been erected. This fence is approximately 9 feet high so a step ladder is required, or a narrow lens required to 'poke' through the gaps. Workings on the new line are also running at the line speed of 125mph. This causes a great deal of turbulence so please be careful.

2) 66414 hauls a 'Malcoms' to Coatbridge.
Jason Rodhouse, September, 12:45, dslr@80mm

Cathiron

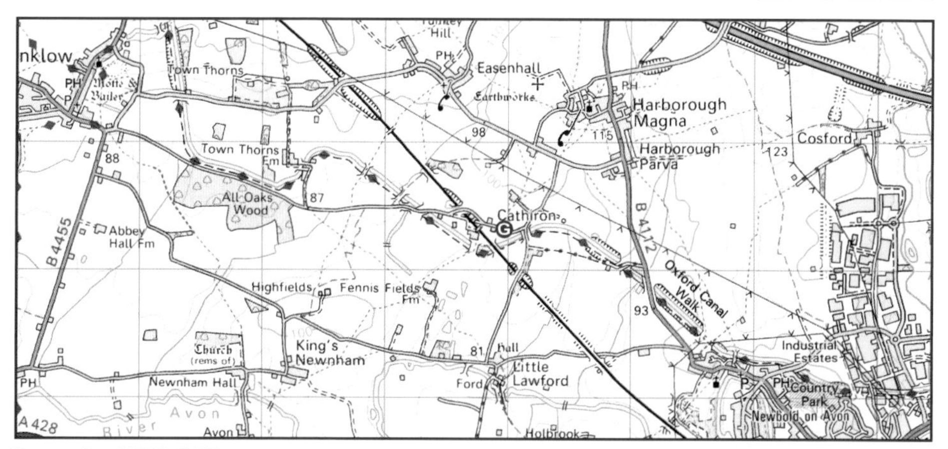

Postcode: CV23 0JH **Lat N52:24:02** **Long W01:18:50**

Road Directions

From M6 Junction 1: take the A426 dual carriageway south and cross over the first four roundabouts. At the fifth take the B4112, second exit or right turn and follow the signs towards Harborough Magna. On the approach to Harborough Magna village you will see a farm on your right. Just after this there is a left turn, Easenhall Road, take this and follow it to the next left which is Cathiron Lane. Take this road. It veers right just before the canal bridge and the location is a few hundred yards further along, where you will see an area of land on the right where you can park.

Please ensure you do not block the driveway.

3) 66434 heads south east towards Rugby, and then on to the DIRFT, with 'Malcoms' from Coatbridge.
June, 17:00, dslr@135mm

Brinklow Loop, Easenhall

Location Notes

This quiet countryside location is between Brinklow and Easenhall just to the north of Rugby. The location itself is at an old footbridge in the middle of the open countryside. It is a footpath linking Stretton under Fosse and Town Thornes.

1) A Virgin Voyager heads south towards Rugby.
Photo by Richard Tearle, July, 13:00, slr@85mm

Public Transport

De Courcey service 585 operates every 30 minutes from Rugby Town Centre to Coventry Railway Station via Brinklow village. Certain journeys (approximately every two hours) also serve Easenhall Village and run along the road between there and Brinklow.

Amenities

None close to hand,

Photographic Notes

There are a number of options from the footbridge. Early on summer mornings you can do southbound shots until around 08.00 from the north side of the bridge. After that you need to move to the south side. Southbounds are then on from the bridge steps or the field till early afternoon. One problem with this shot is that freight is often 'looped' here at the signal just to the north. Although slow moving freight is good for the northbound shot this will block any southbound movements whilst the train is paused.
Early summer shots are best at this location before line-side growth becomes too tall, otherwise a step ladder is highly recommended for the fence line shots.

2) 66092 heads south, with a short engineers train.
Photo by Jason Rodhouse, October, 13:30, dslr@35mm

3) 66416 with the 'Malcoms' intermodal heads south.
Photo by Jason Rodhouse, April, 16:00, dslr@18mm

Brinklow Loop, Easenhall

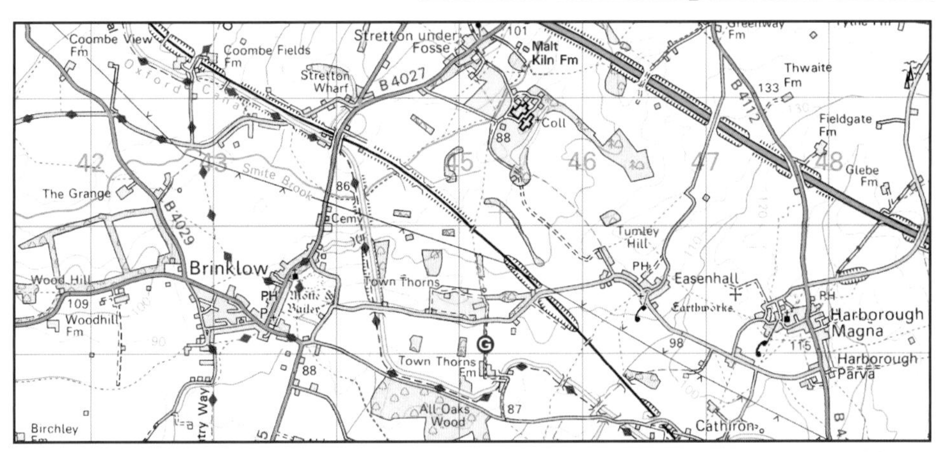

Postcode: CV23 0JE **Lat N52:24:57** **Long W01:20:17**

Road Directions

From Rugby, take the B4112 through Newbold towards Harborough Magna. As you approach Harborough Magna, take a left turn to Easenhall, looking out for 'The White Horse' on the right. Carry on through Easenhall village, and you will soon cross the railway. Continue along the road to 'Ben' Town Thornes Nursing Home on the right. There is plenty of room to park on the road side opposite the nursing home. From these grounds follow the public footpath, through two gates and turn left through a gap in the trees to reach the location. The walk will take 5 to 10 minutes.

4) With 86623 leading 86610 heads north with a liner for Coatbridge.
Photo by Jason Rodhouse, July 15:45, dslr@56mm

Shilton, Oxford Canal

Location Notes

A classic shot of the West Coast Main line opposite the Oxford Canal. It is very open and exposed to the elements with very little shelter and it is quite a walk back to the car.

1) GBRf 66713 heads south with a Hams Hall to Felixstowe intermodal.
Photo by Jason Rodhouse, February. 14:45, dslr@24mm

The location has picked up the tag of Ansty, in fact the location is only a couple of hundred yards from the former Shilton station.

Public Transport

De Courcey Travel services 74/75 operate hourly between Coventry and Nuneaton via Ansty and Shilton. You can alight in either village and then walk to the location.

2) A northbound DRS loco move with 47802 & 37038.
Photo by Jason Rodhouse, March, 16:00, dslr@24mm

Amenities

There are pubs in both Shilton and Ansty villages. Bulkington, which is about three miles away, has a chip shop. There is also a McDonalds on the A4600 into Coventry, about two miles away.

Photographic Notes

The location favours mid afternoon shots as it is only by this time that the sun has come round to be on the right side and on the nose for northbound workings. However the light remains good right up to sunset as there is little in the way of hills to the west to cast shadows. There is also a window of opportunity for southbound workings, between about 11.00 and 13.00. A new telephone point has been installed by the lineside which narrows the field of view of this shot. If you are really lucky you might get a passing canal boat at the same time as a passing train.
During the summer months the vegetation between the canal and line can encroach on shots.

Shilton, Oxford Canal

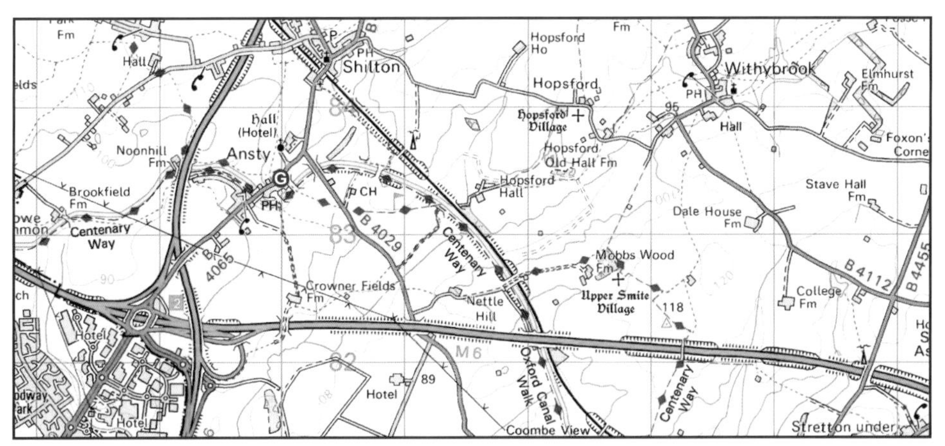

Postcode: CV7 9HZ **Lat N52:26:38** **Long W01:23:29**

Road Directions

From M6 junction 2: take the B4065 north, signposted Shilton and Ansty. After about 1 mile turn right on the B4029, signposted 'Ansty Golf Club'. Take this road and then either park on the Oxford Canal bridge and make your way down to the towpath and walk along to the location; or drive furtrher down the B4029 and park by the set of metal gates protecting a field, taking care not to obstruct the gates and walk across the track in the field to reach the location. Both routes are likely to be problematic after wet weather.

3) 56312 & 56311 head north with the 1200 MThO Dollands Moor-Hams Hall.
Photo by Scott Borthwick, September, 17:30, slr@38mm

Church Lawford, Coventry Road

Location Notes

Church Lawford is a village on the outskirts of Rugby. The location is open fields bordering the line.

1) With the afternoon Birmingham trip 90018 heads north with WB64, in old Virgin Trains colours, in tow.
Photo by Jason Rodhouse, March, 16:00, dslr@34mm

Public Transport

Stagecoach service 86 operates from Rugby to Coventry and calls at both Long Lawford and Church Lawford Villages, from where you can walk back to the location.

Amenities

There is nothing at the location, but nearby Long Lawford has a Co-op mini supermarket and a few pubs. There is also a very good pub in Church Lawford, 'The Old Smithy'. Further down in the village, towards Kings Newnham, is a Wyevale Garden Centre on the left. This has a cafe which makes fresh sandwiches and snacks.

2) 92030 with a late running Bescot to Wembley enterprise with 92042, 66027 and 66207 in tow.
Photo by Jason Rodhouse, March, 18:15, dslr@50mm

Photographic Notes

The line here runs pretty much east to west so lighting is not normally a problem. You can access fields on both the north and south of the line so well lit shots should be available throughout the day. Also the nearby Rugby Cement works can provide an interesting feature on the skyline of east facing shots. Though not especially busy, the noise from the A428 (Coventry Road) does not make this an ideal location for video, especially if shooting from the southern side of the line.

3) 67017 leads a Victoria to Runcorn VSOE charter.
Photo by Jason Rodhouse, March, 09:45, dslr@39mm

Church Lawford, Coventry Road

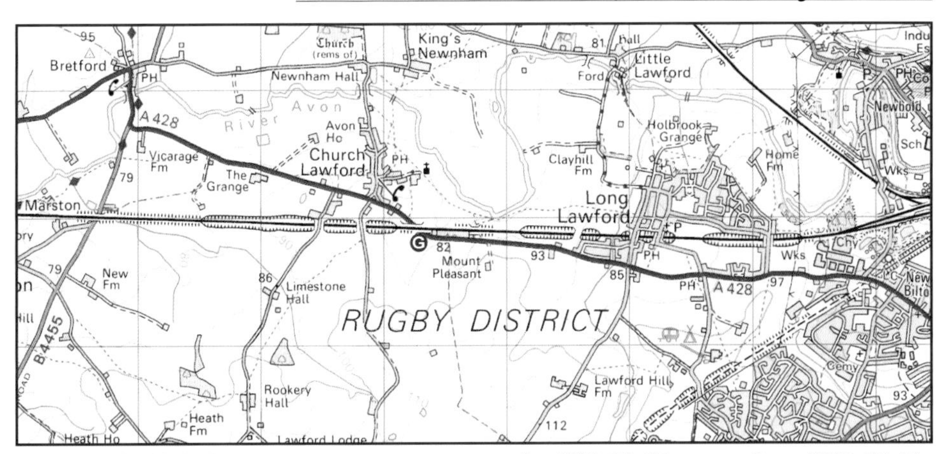

Postcode: CV23 9EJ **Lat N52:22:47** **Long W01:19:46**

Road Directions

From Rugby, take the A428 towards Coventry, passing through the village of Long Lawford. You should soon notice the railway line on your right, running parallel with the road. The next village is Church Lawford but you need to make a right hand turn before you reach this village. This turning is shortly before the road alters direction and goes under the railway, and is directly opposite Mount Pleasant. As you make this turn, you should see a bridge carrying the railway line directly in front of you and a small works plant to your left.

You can park on the right, just opposite the works plant. There are enough spaces here for several cars. Walk under the bridge to reach the field location.

4) 66054 heads east with a Coventry Prologis to Wembley empty cargowagons move.
Photo by Jason Rodhouse, April, 12:15, dslr@36mm

Bicester to Birmingham

Passenger Traffic

A number of passenger operators use this line. Chiltern Railways operates mainly between Marylebone and Birmingham Snow Hill. In addition to this a few trains branch off at Hatton and terminate at Stratford-upon-Avon. The trains are formed of 165 and 168 Diesel Multiple Units.

1) 67025 top and tails with 67013 with an afternoon Wrexham and Shropshire working through Hatton.
Photo by Scott Borthwick, September, 17:00, slr@45mm

Wrexham and Shropshire also operate out of Marylebone using DB Schenker 67 and MkIII coaches and DVTs. The loco usually being on the London end of the train. The early morning workings run via Tyseley and Hatton. The rest via Coventry. A third operator, Cross Country also uses the route with 220/221 DEMUs

Freight Traffic

DB Schenker and Freightliner Intermodal traffic dominate the route with motive power provided by class 66s from both operators.
A small number of coal and oil workings are also scheduled, with the coal going to Didcot Power Station and the oil going to Theale. The oil workings will often produce a class 60.
There is also a weekly Colas Steel train from Burton on Trent to the Channel Tunnel.

Occasional Traffic

The odd Serco test train traverses the route, as well as plenty of tours. There are often steam workings from Tyseley to various destinations.

2) 66589 with an intermodal at Cropredy.
Photo by Jason Rodhouse, July, 15:15, dslr@200mm

3) 50049 & 031 pass Bishops Itchington with a charter.
Photo by Scott Borthwick, March, 12:00, slr@70mm

Bicester to Birmingham

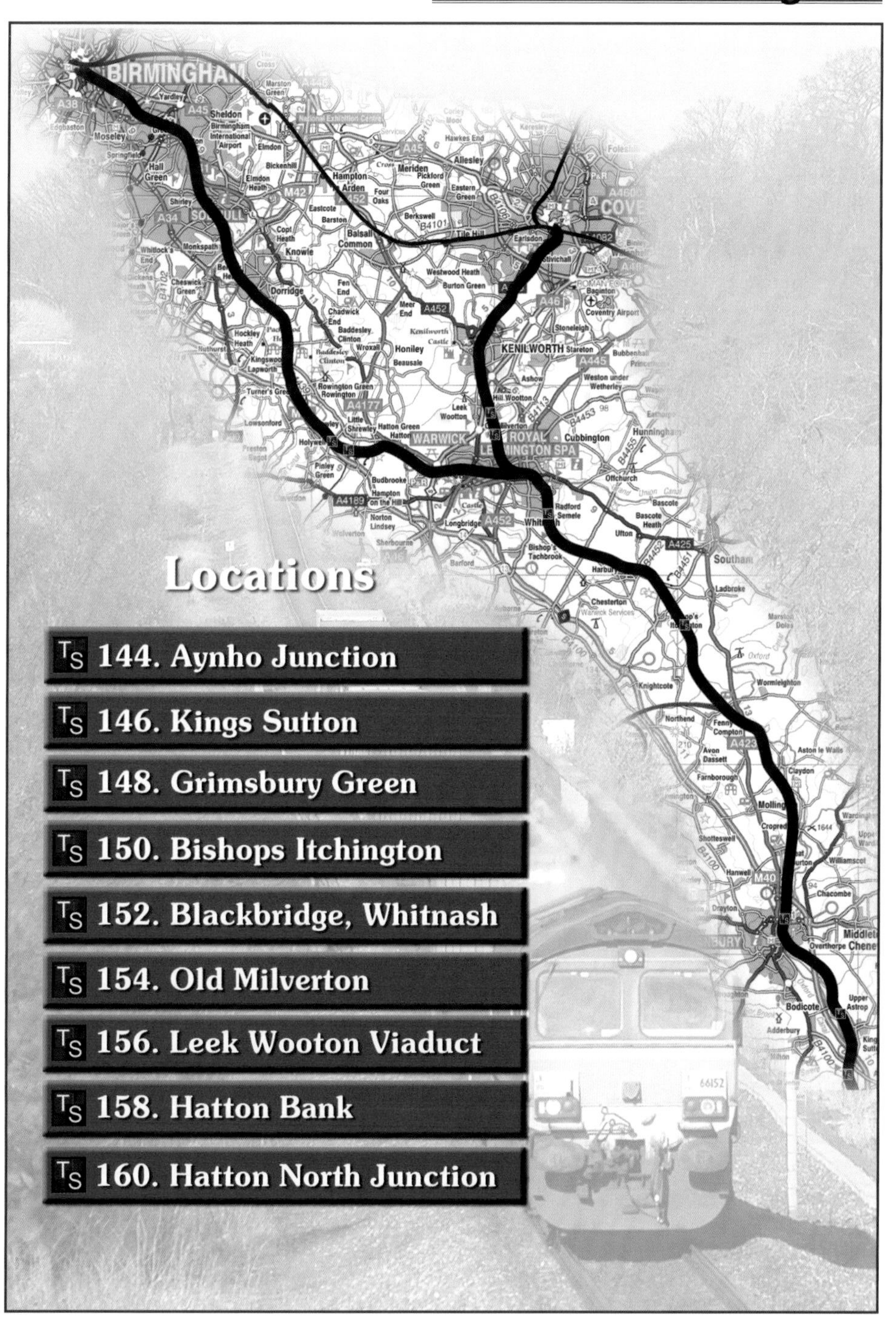

Aynho Junction

Location Notes

Aynho is a pleasant Northamptonshire village which is close to the Oxfordshire border. The location itself is an overbridge on the line running between Banbury and Oxford. The road can often be busy, so be vigilant. And although there is no pavement, there is room to stand 'off the road' on either side of the bridge on the grass verges.

1) In the early morning summer sun D444 heads north with a Bristol to Aberystwyth charter.
Photo by Richard Tearle, May, 06:15, slr@135mm

Public Transport

SMS Executive Travel service 499 runs bi-hourly from Banbury Bus station to Anyho village. From there walk west down Station Road to reach the location.

Amenities

'The Great Western Arms' is right next to the location - and they do serve food.

2) A solo 168 heads along the line towards Aylesbury.
Photo by Jason Rodhouse, November, 15:15, dslr@38mm

Photographic Notes

Early afternoon light is best for southbound trains but be wary of the shadow from the station building creeping in, especially when the sun is low.
A telephoto lens, although not vital, would provide more photographic opportunities here.
The B4031 bridge can be very busy with road traffic, and the nearby M40 makes video recordings difficult at this location.

Aynho Junction

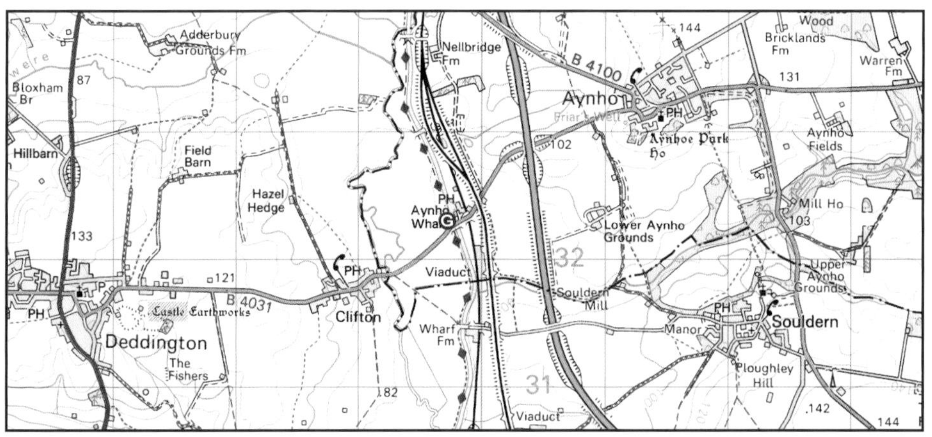

Postcode: OX17 3BP **Lat N51:59:14** **Long W01:16:29**

Road Directions

From M40 Junction 10: exit on the A43 towards Brckley. After about ¾ mile turn left on the B4100. Continue for about 5 miles and turn left on the B4031. This will take you under the motorway to the location.

Do not park in the pub car park unless you are going to be having food or drinks there. However, there is room to park several cars on the grass verge by the bridge. Alternatively, there are parking spaces immediately before the motorway bridge, on the left.

3) 47727 and 748 pass the old station with the Thursdays only Burton-upon-Trent to Dollands Moor steel working.
Photo by Scott Borthwick, July, 15:30, slr@35mm

Kings Sutton

Location Notes

A road overbridge and footpath crossing with a well recognised view of the Kings Sutton Church Spire. The location is very popular on late summer afternoons and evenings, which is by far the best time for photography as the steeple on the village church is often illuminated by lovely evening sunlight.

1) WSMR DVT 82301 is pushed past the distinctive spire with an afternoon Marylebone to Wrexham service.
Photo by Chris Nevard, May, 17:45, dslr@50mm

Public Transport

The road bridge is about a 20 minute walk from Kings Sutton station which is served approximately hourly from Marylebone and two hourly from Oxford. There are two routes to walk from the station to the bridge, one through the village and along the roads, the other via a public footpath through fields and across the line at a foot crossing midway between the station and the bridge.
Theses fields are flood plains so they are easily flooded. Following wet weather, the road route is highly recommended.

2) 47749 heads south with a Colas steel working.
Photo by Richard Tearle, May, 15:30 slr@85mm

Amenities

There is a Co-op in Kings Sutton village.

Photographic Notes

Although shots of southbound trains are possible earlier in the day, the shot of choice is the late afternoon/evening northbound shot.
It should also be noted that shots are obtainable from the field on the west side of the line in both directions and from a crossing further south. If choosing these options please try to ensure you are not in the shots of anyone shooting from the bridge.

3) 67010 on a WSMR football special to Wembley.
Photo by Geoff Plumb, May, 11:15, dslr@58mm

Kings Sutton

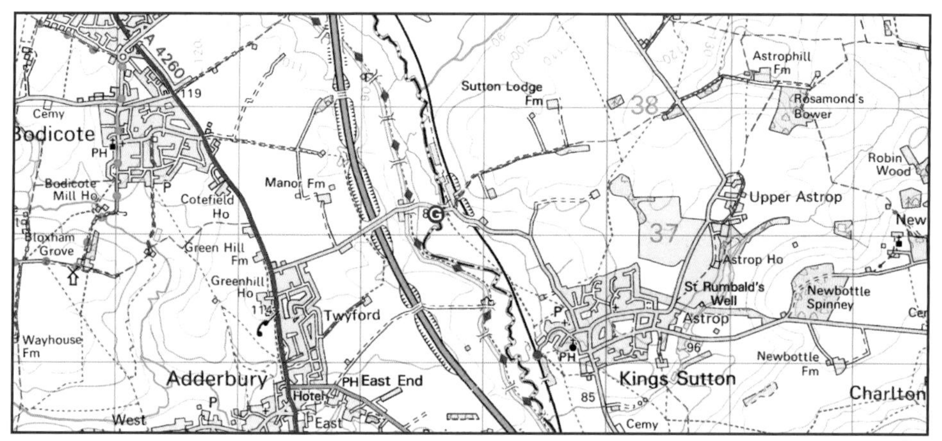

Postcode: OX17 3AA **Lat N52:01:48** **Long W01:17:20**

Road Directions

Take the A4260 (Oxford Road) south out of Banbury. Turn left at the road signposted 'Kings Sutton' and follow this road down the hill to the Cherwell Valley grain stores. Here the road turns to the right.

Park in the field entrance on the right ensuring you maintain access for farm traffic as, although the field is generally fallow, it is still used. There is room for about 4 cars.

4) 66541 heads north at Kings Sutton with a Southampton to Trafford Park intermodal.
Photo by Scott Borthwick, June, 19:15, dlsr@30mm

Grimsbury Green, Banbury

Location Notes

This location is a relatively quiet road bridge on the outskirts of Banbury, a large town in Oxfordshire.

1) 47749 and 739 haul the Burton to Dollands Moor steel working south.
Photo by Jason Rodhouse, May, 09:15, dslr@135mm

Public Transport

The location is about a 10 minute walk along Cherwell Street and Concord Avenue from Banbury railway station.

Amenities

There are no amenities at the location itself but in the town centre you will find most things. The 'Right Plaice' in Broad Street is highly recommended if you like fish and chips.

Photographic Notes

Due to the main road bridge just to the south, photographs of northbound workings can be ruled out almost completely. The space between the two bridges does not allow for anything more than a side on snap shot.

Facing north, there is little to cast shadows so you can choose a side throughout most of the day.

Due to the busy roads and motorway nearby, this location is not suitable for audio recordings.

The nearby 'La Farge' site can make an interesting backdrop!

2) 66114 heads south on a loaded intermodal past the La Farge works.
Photo by Jason Rodhouse, April, 15:00, dslr@45mm

Grimsbury Green, Banbury

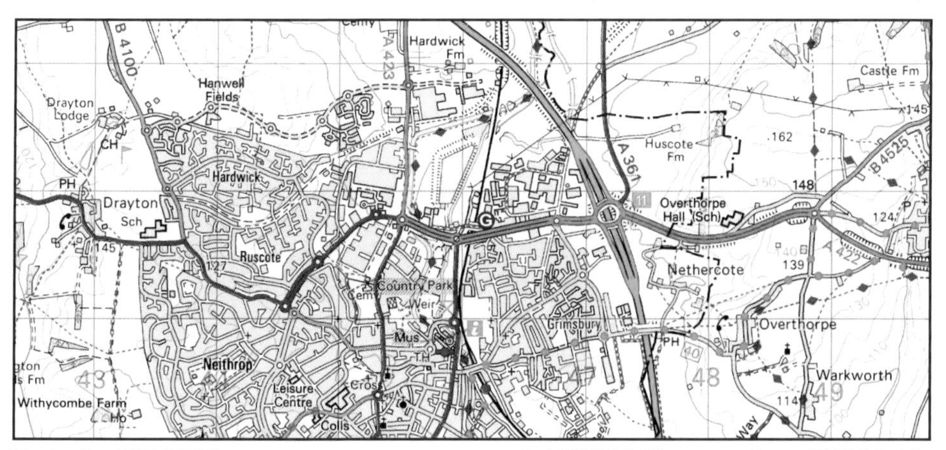

Postcode: OX16 3JX **Lat N52:04:20** **Long W01:19:44**

Road Directions

From M40 Junction 11: head towards Banbury town centre. Go straight over the first roundabout and turn right at the second. You should notice signs for Grimsbury Manor and also a sign for a sailing/boating club. Bear right and park by the bridge.

There is ample room here to park several cars which would be in view at all times.

3) 37602 and 069 head south with 'The Wessexman' Spitfire Charter from Crewe to Weymouth.
Photo by Richard Tearle, May, 09:15, slr@135mm

Bishops Itchington, Holmes House Farm

Location Notes

The location is a quiet overbridge in a rural location. Bishops Itchington is a Warwickshire village between nearby Leamington Spa and Southam. The location is about a mile to the south of the village.

1) 66054 heads up a northbound intermodal to Hams Hall.
Photo by Jason Rodhouse, June, 14:15, dslr@28mm

Be aware that the farmer often moves cattle down the lane, so damage could be caused to your car.

Public Transport

Stagecoach service 64 operates hourly from Leamington Spa to Bishops Itchington village, from where it would be about a 25-30 minute walk to the location.

Amenities

There are a couple of shops in the village where snacks can be purchased. Real ale fans may want to try the 'Butchers Arms' in Fisher Street, or the 'Great Western'.

Photographic Notes

Shots can be taken from both sides of the bridge. Trains coming from the south can be seen a considerable distance away, which should make for good video.
The bridge sides directly over the rail lines are quite high, but the edges are a comfortable height to photograph from without the need for a step ladder.

Bishops Itchington, Holmes House Farm

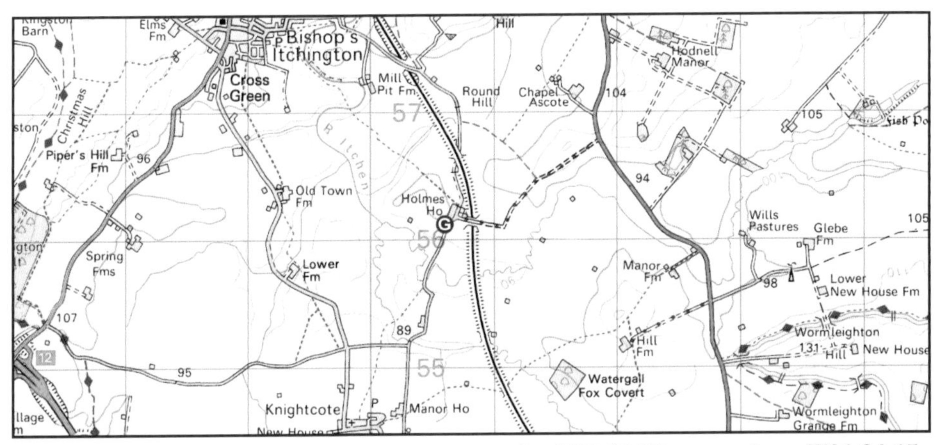

Postcode: CV47 2SB **Lat N52:12:08** **Long W01:24:15**

Road Directions

From M40 Junction 12: take the B4451 north east to Bishops Itchington. In the village, turn right down either Fisher Road or Chapel Street, and continue to the bottom of the village via Poplar Road. Turn into Hambridge Road and follow it over a bridge crossing the line, then soon afterwards passing under it. Shortly after this, you will see a farm house on the right. The location is down the lane immediately opposite.

You can park opposite the farmhouse, or on the bridge itself. If parking on the bridge, please park to one side so the farmer can pass if he needs to. You may find it easier to reverse the short distance down the lane, as turning can be difficult if you actually cross the bridge.

2) 67014 heads to London with a staff special for Wrexham and Shropshire prior to the start of their timetabled service.
Photo by Scott Borthwick, April, 10:45, slr@35mm

Blackbridge, Whitnash

Location Notes

The location is a quiet overbridge near the church yard, between a housing estate and some playing fields. It is right on the edge of the town and there is open countryside to the east. Whitnash is now effectively a suburb of Royal Leamington Spa.

2) 66024 with a southbound intermodal to Southampton.
Photo by Jason Rodhouse, May, 18:30, dslr@65mm

Public Transport

Stagecoach's G1 service runs between Warwick, Leamington Spa and Whitnash during the day.

Amenities

There is a pub and a few local shops off St. Margarets Road, There is also a good selection of shops and a Supermarket in nearby Sydenham, with many more in Leamington Spa.

Accommodation

There is a range of hotels and Bed and Breakfasts in Leamington Spa, including a Holiday Inn on the nearby industrial estate and a Travel Inn on the A46.

Photographic Notes

The line runs almost north to south at this location so it is best for southbound trains after mid morning. The bridge sides are quite high so a step ladder will be an advantage for some.

1) 60074 works a northbound oil train to Lindsey.
Jason Rodhouse, May, 18:30, dslr@65mm

Blackbridge, Whitnash

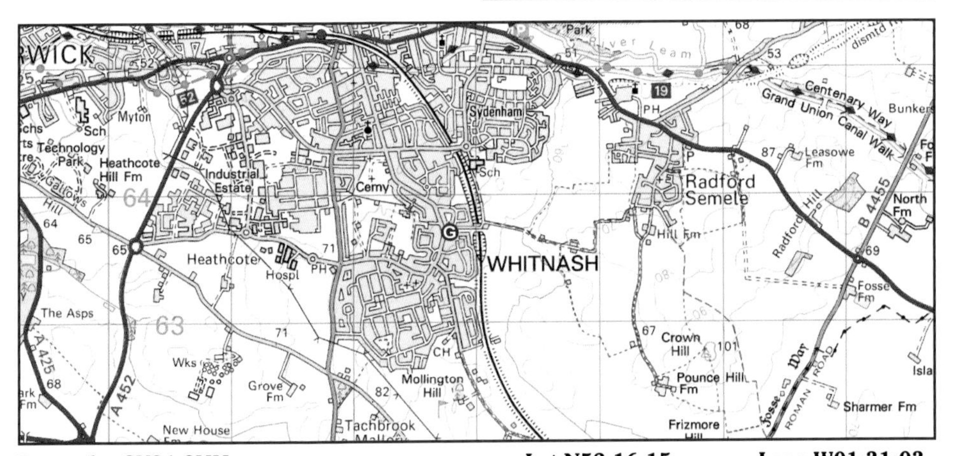

Postcode: CV31 2HH **Lat N52:16:15** **Long W01:31:03**

Road Directions

From Leamington station: head south on the Tachbrook road. When you come to the crossroads, turn left into St. Helens Road, follow this road, passing the Cemetery on the right, until you come to a turning on the right which you will need to take (Brunswick Street) Follow this road, and look out for Church Lane on your left. This is the lane which leads to the location.

There is room to park by the churchyard, or if this is busy, you can park on the opposite side of the bridge but do not block the gates.

3) 67014 heads to London with a staff special for Wrexham and Shropshire working prior to the start of their timetable.
Photo by Scott Borthwick, April, 15:30, slr@45mm

Old Milverton

Location Notes

A quiet countryside location on the outskirts of Leamington Spa and Warwick. The location is actually two bridges within close proximity. The southern is a public footpath, the northern, a road bridge.

1) 67014 top and tails with 67012 on the first northbound revenue earning service to Wrexham,
Photo by Scott Borthwick, April, 08:15, slr@33mm

Public Transport

Flexibus service 506 runs once a day from Leamington Spa to Old Milverton telephone box which is opposite the northern road, bridge.

Amenities

There is a useful shop on the main road in Old Milverton. Nearby Warwick and Leamington Spa can cater for all needs.

Photographic Notes

The road bridge offers a long straight view towards Kenilworth and the footbridge views towards Leamington. When the sun is low this can sometimes be a problem on the footpath bridge as shadows of the lineside trees can be very long. You will not have this problem from the road bridge.
Noise should not be a problem for those taking video at the footbridge, although sometimes aircraft to and from Coventry airport can be heard. On both sides of the location the track climbs so locomotives should be working to haul trains up the inclines.
Shots can be taken from both sides and at various angles from both bridges. Given the straight nature of the track at location it is well suited to telephoto shots. On the road bridge there is no pavement, only a reasonably wide grass verge.

2) Southbound 66152 tackles the climb to Milverton.
Photo by Pauline McKenna, Feb, 12:30, dslr@200mm

Old Milverton

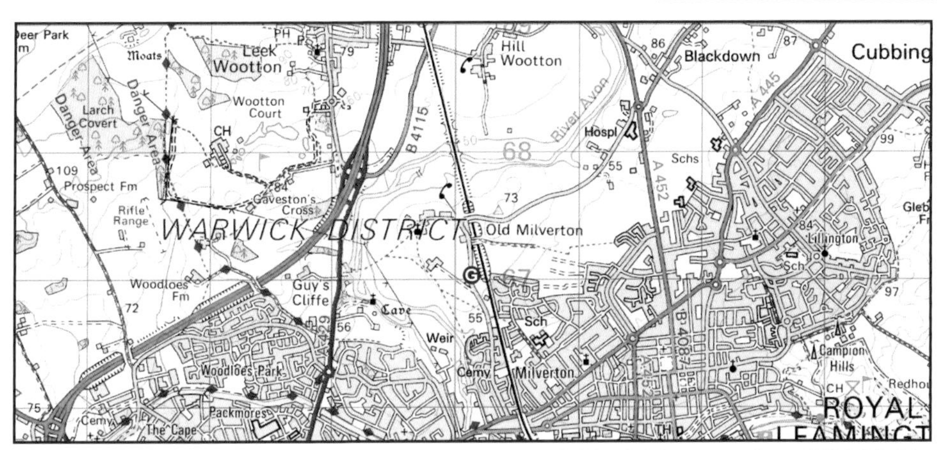

Postcode: CV32 6SA **Lat N52:18:11** **Long W01:33:31**

Road Directions

From M40 Junction 15 (Warwick): head north on the A429. Keep on this road through Warwick. You will pass under a railway bridge and shortly after will see another road bridge ahead. Turn left before this second bridge. The road is clearly signposted for 'Old Milverton'. Follow this speed hump ridden road until you have passed the housing estate and there are allotments to your right. Just before you come to the first dwelling on the left the 'public footpath' bridge is on your right.

Continue and you will see a left hand turn to the church as the main road bears right. Follow the road to the right and pull up almost immediately on the left just before the road bridge. This is the second location - there is ample parking, and it is a short walk between the bridges.

3) 66034 climbs up the incline towards Coventry with a late running, northbound, intermodal to Birch Coppice.
Photo by Jason Rodhouse, April, 16:15, dslr@300mm

Leek Wootton Viaduct

Location Notes

This location is a low viaduct across the River Avon in open countryside and farm land.

1) An XC Voyager as seen from the north west side of the viaduct.
July, 09:15, dslr@24mm

Public Transport

Stagecoach service 16 operates hourly between Coventry, Kenilworth, Warwick, Leamington Spa and Stratford upon Avon and stops in Leek Wootton village. Walk south out of the village towards the A46. Go under the road and the you should be able to see the viaduct across the fields.

Amenities

There are none at the location but Warwick and Royal Leamington Spa have a very wide range of shops.

Photographic Notes

There are angles on most sides of the viaduct. Most are looking down the gently sloping sides of the Avon river valley or you can head down to the river and go for side-on shots.
There is a kink in the river which allows the photographer to shoot trains on the viaduct across the water. The wall on the viaduct has been replaced by railings on the west side, thus making the wheels of trains visible. There are some electric wires on the east side which can intrude into your shot.
In addition to the side-on shot of the train crossing the water, it is possible to go further up the field and tighter in to the viaduct in order to photograph trains crossing the viaduct with the whole train in the shot. Video pan shots of trains crossing the entire viaduct are possible here. The location is well away from any roads so road noise is not a problem.

Leek Wootton Viaduct

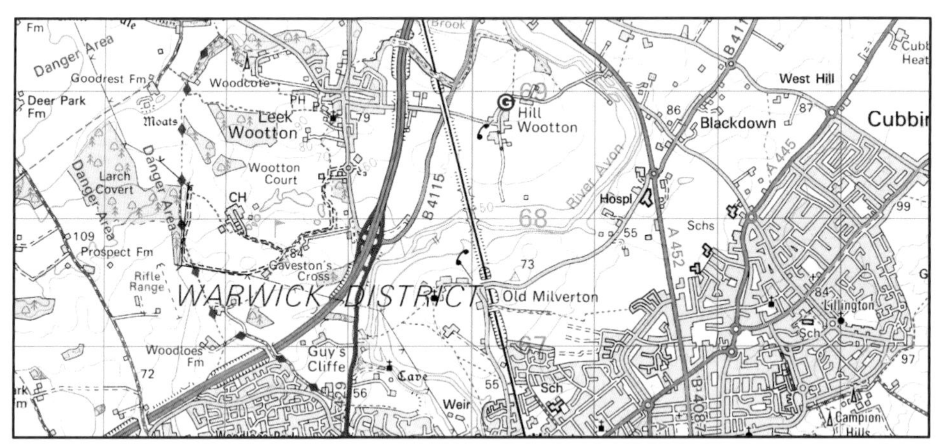

Postcode: CV35 7PP **Lat N52:18:35** **Long W01:33:46**

Road Directions

For the north side: leave the A46 at the B4115. After about a quarter of a mile there is a gated entrance to your right, the third right turn, on the brow of a hill. Park here (without blocking the gateway) and walk across the fields to the viaduct. You can also walk under the line to access the north east side. The first gate only leads into a field with a narrow angle on the viaduct.

For the south side: leave the A46 at the B4115. When you go under the railway line turn right towards Hill Wootton. Follow this road through the village and at the T-junction turn right. Take the third exit at the roundabout - towards Old Milverton. Just before the 'Old Milverton' village signs there is a field entrance on the right. Park here, but do not block the entrance. From here you can walk down the side of the field to the grass lands and walk under the viaduct if required. This is the better location for side-on shots of the viaduct.

Both walks involve crossing farm land so treat the land with respect and if it has been raining, wear suitable footwear.

2) With 'The Irish Mail' D1015 crosses the viaduct on the way to Holyhead, viewed from the north east side.
Photo by John Deeming, February, 09:15, dslr@36mm

Hatton Bank

Location Notes

A rural location in South Warwickshire to the north of Leamington Spa. The location is a field, often used by walkers and horse riders.

1) Castle 5043 Earl of Mount Edgcumbe and Hall 4965 Rood Ashton Hall passing the bridge as they head towards Didcot. *Photo by David Dawson, November, 11:45, dslr@40mm*

Public Transport

Hatton Station is approximately a 20-30 minute walk along the canal from the locations and is well served by trains from Marylebone, Birmingham and Stratford upon Avon.

Amenities

There is a little cafe by the canal car park. It is open weekdays and weekends and does good cooked breakfasts, lunches etc. The cafe has toilet facilities. You can also sit outside and keep an eye on what is passing along the line.
'The Waterman' pub is just along the main road.

2) 66117 works a Southampton to Burton 'modal'. *Photo by Jason Rodhouse, November, 11:45, dslr@30mm*

Photographic Notes

Both northbound and southbound shots are available. Southbound shots are favourable until around lunchtime, with northbound shots after that until early evening.
Whilst a step ladder is by no means essential at the footpath locations, you may find it gives you some extra height, especially in the summer when the vegetation on the banks can grow quite high.
This is an ideal location for video as there is very little noise. It is however, quite open to wind.
The background in view 3 has changed slightly since the picture was taken as there is now a signal gantry in the distance. But this should not have any great impact.

Hatton Bank

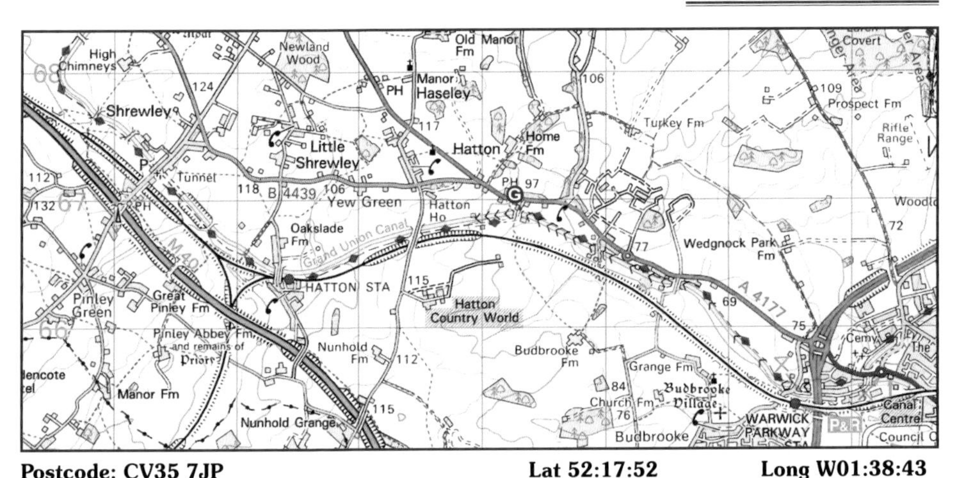

Postcode: CV35 7JP **Lat 52:17:52** **Long W01:38:43**

Road Directions

From the A46 (Warwick Bypass): take the A4177 towards Solihull. After passing a new housing development on the right you start to climb gently. Look out for the signposted entrance, on the left, to a British Waterways compound that has a public car park. Enter this and park the car here. Cross the canal bridge and a public footpath leads across the field to the footbridge over the railway line. After the bridge, a footpath leads along the edge of the field. Although not marked as a footpath, this is a nature trail for the nearby Hatton Country World. After crossing the style, walk uphill and you will see a number of shots, depending on the height of the vegetation.

The British Waterways car park is pay and display and costs £1.20. The car park closes at 17.30 in winter and 21.00 in Summer.

3) 66044 climbs the bank with a Fawley to Washwood Heath 'sticky tanks' working.
Photo by Scott Borthwick, June, 18:45, slr@41mm

Hatton North Junction

Location Notes

A little used footbridge which crosses the line in rural surroundings. This is also the junction where the line goes down to Stratford-upon-Avon, although trains from Stratford-upon-Avon travelling towards Leamington will emerge from the other end of the junction which is not visible here.

1) 168218 heads north towards Birmingham with a working from London Marylebone.
Photo by Jason Rodhouse, June, 14:40, dslr@42mm

Public Transport

The location is a 15-20 minute walk along the canal towpath from Hatton Station. The footpath leading to the location is close to the bridge over the canal, but is quite overgrown so would be difficult in wet weather.

Amenities

The post office and shop in Shrewley may be of use. There is also the 'Durham Ox' restaurant and pub on the main road.

Accomodation

'The Haseley Coach House Motel' is a few miles away and there are plenty of options in Warwick or Royal Leamington Spa.

Photographic Notes

A good selection of shots from different angles can be had here but the shot of choice has to be of westbound workings between around 14.00 and 18.00. You can either shoot from the bridge steps or from the side of the field which is on a raised embankment.
The constant noise from the M40 might not make this location suitable for video.

Hatton North Junction

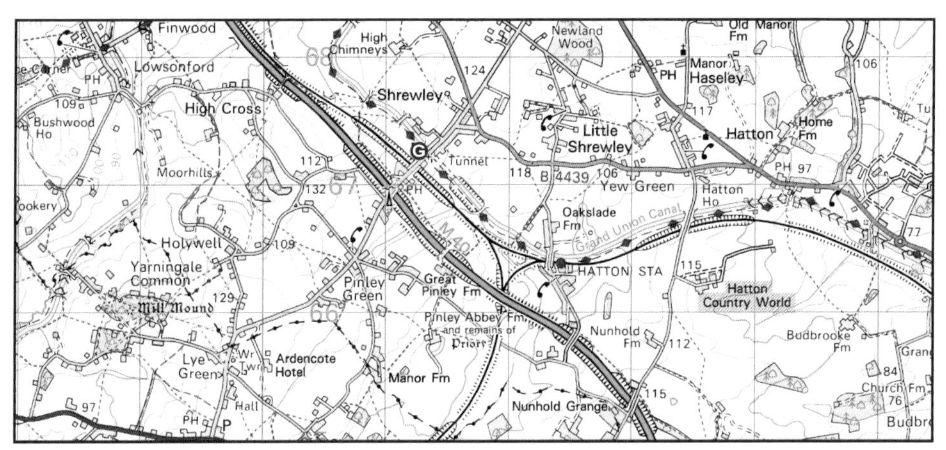

Postcode: CV35 7AN **Lat N52:17:50** **Long W01:40:57**

Road Directions

From the Warwick bypass (A46): take the A4177 towards Solihull. Keep on this road until you can take the B4439 to Shrewley. As you approach Shrewley take the left hand spur. If you miss it, simply take the next left at the junction. Park near the post office.

Walk back towards the motorway and just before you reach it there is a footpath. Cross the style and walk round the field edges to the location. The walk should take about 15 minutes from the post office.

2) 66305 passes Hatton North Junction with an unidentified empty coal working.
Photo by Jason Rodhouse, September, 16:30, dslr@xxmm

Photo by Albert Dawson